A HOMEMADE CHRISTMAS

HARLEQUIN®

A Homemade Christmas

ISBN: 978-0-373-89222-8

Library of Congress Cataloging-in-Publication Data

Barseghian, Tina.
  A homemade Christmas / Tina Barseghian.
    p. cm.
  Includes bibliographical references and index.
  ISBN 978-0-373-89222-8 (pbk.)
  1. Christmas decorations. 2. Handicraft. 3. Christmas cookery. I. Title.
  TT900.C4B425 2010
  745.594'12--dc22

                                    2009051942

www.eharlequin.com
Printed in Singapore.

A HOMEMADE CHRISTMAS

Creative Ideas for an Earth-Friendly, Frugal, Festive Holiday

Tina Barseghian

Illustrations by Alison Kendall

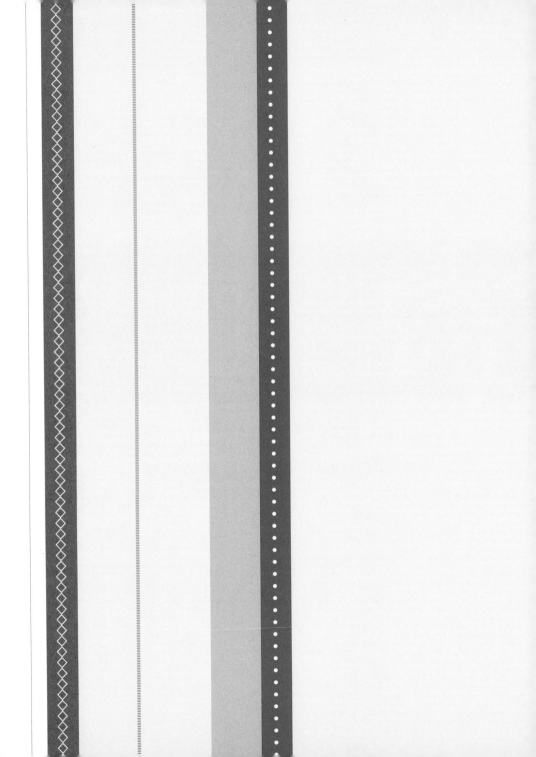

CONTENTS

INTRODUCTION

The idea of a homemade holiday sounds appealing: taking the time to create handcrafted gifts and decorations, making home-baked goodies, and enjoying quality time with family. But too often, our busy and over-committed schedules don't allow us to slow down. Our consumer culture encourages us to spend the holidays in a frenzy of wasteful buying and materialism, and the countdown to Christmas becomes fraught with expense and anxiety instead of fun and anticipation. This book is intended to help you find a new approach—to break the cycle and create a meaningful, modern, family- and earth-friendly homemade holiday.

❈

The philosophy behind *A Homemade Christmas* is simple: Giving part of yourself—your time, efforts, and talent—will help you get into the genuine holiday spirit. And with personal gestures that come straight from the heart—by way of a handmade gift or a home cooked meal— you'll not only discover new holiday meaning, you'll also demonstrate your appreciation for those you love. Involve family members, including kids, friends, and even colleagues, in your plan to have a homemade Christmas.

✳

But rest assured, a homemade Christmas does not require an inordinate amount of extra time, it does not call for much financial outlay, and you don't have to be a highly skilled crafter or cook. All you need to do is make the choice that this year you're going to take a new approach to the holiday revelry. Relax, step away from the frenzy, and head into this Christmas season with the knowledge that it's all about your attitude.

✳

A Homemade Christmas shows you how to take back the holidays with an easy-to-follow blueprint for adding a homemade touch to everything you do. You'll find it's not only easier than you thought, but also much more enjoyable. Each of the five chapters in this book covers one aspect of traditional Christmas celebrations and provides a wealth of ideas, projects, tips, and advice for going homemade.

Greeting: The holidays offer a great opportunity each year to reach out to friends and family. Here are a number of ideas to create personal, artful cards that are also green, quick, and fun to make.

✺

Trimming: Express yourself and show some flair by decorating your home and trimming your tree. This chapter is packed with ideas for making decorations and ornaments, projects for handmade embellishments, suggestions for quick homemade touches, and earth-friendly tips.

✺

Cooking: Delicious meals, delectable sweets, mouth-watering aromas wafting from the kitchen—holiday cooking is the very essence of Christmas. Here are simple suggestions for cooking and sharing the bounty of the kitchen.

✺

Giving: It's the heart of the holiday spirit. Find creative ways to put your talents to use in this chapter. Choose from a variety of clever ideas and easy instructions for handcrafted presents and thoughtful alternatives for gifts that draw on your unique skills and enthusiasms.

✳

Celebrating: Traditions give the holidays context and meaning, and draw people together. This chapter offers ideas for creating new traditions, cementing old ones, and making connections with the community.

✳

Children's uninhibited joy is what makes Christmas delightful for everyone, so within each chapter we offer suggestions for kid-friendly projects, ways to include little ones in your preparations, and ideas for fun, homemade family activities. You'll also see the recurring theme of finding ways to green your holidays with eco-conscious choices.

✳

We hope the ideas in *A Homemade Christmas* inspire you with a sense of renewal to enjoy the holiday.

chapter

GREETING

Share the Christmas spirit with heartfelt holiday greetings.

The holidays provide the perfect occasion to send warm wishes to all those we care about. Busy months speed by, and between work, school, travel, and the distractions of life, we may not have the time or opportunity to reach out and catch up with friends and family as much as we'd like.

*

But the holidays give us the opportunity to slow down and take the time to make and send personal greetings. With written notes and photos, we bring people back into our lives. The process of deciding on the idea of the card, assembling the elements, and writing a heartfelt message connects you to your loved ones, showing them that they're on your mind and that they mean a lot to you.

*

It's also a way for you to express yourself artistically—even if you don't necessarily think of yourself as a visual artist. Homemade holiday greetings can take the form of art, collage, photos, videos, essays—or whatever appeals to you and works within your budget and time constraints.

*

"Homemade" in this context means that you put some of your own handiwork into creating your greeting—but it does not have to mean that you must create each element from scratch, eschew technology, or reject anything manufactured. The effort you make and the personal connection you forge in sending the greeting are what make it special. A holiday card amid the stack of catalogs and bills is sure to be the first piece of mail opened; a personal message in your email in-box (especially if it comes complete with photos or video) will be opened with equal anticipation.

*

This chapter offers homemade greeting ideas for every level of time and skill. If you're excited to exercise your crafty muscles, you may enjoy making your own stamps, creating collages with different types of media, or embroidering a Christmas message. If your time is very limited or your skills more technical than crafty, you can create a different type of homemade greeting: check out the section on digital greetings, consider writing a holiday blog, or use your camera to make a video. Making holiday cards is a great activity to share with children, too. There are also plenty of suggestions for reusing, recycling, and repurposing materials to help make your Christmas greetings earth-friendly.

*

Reach out and connect with your friends and family, and get yourself ready to enjoy the holidays!

Send a Photo Card

Embellishments make photo cards extra-special.

During the year, we rarely have the opportunity to share print photos with our friends and family. Most of us have gone fully digital and have learned to negotiate the digital process: download photos from the camera, upload them to photo-sharing websites, and send the links to our loved ones. If we're lucky, we can pull this off a few times a year.

Seeing the images online is fun, but it doesn't give the same satisfaction as holding an actual printed photograph in your hand. There's the delicious anticipation upon spotting the envelope in your mailbox, followed by the thrill of opening it and seeing the photo for the first time: the children's goofy smiles, the pet's hilarious outfit, your friend sipping a margarita in Mexico. Stick it on the fridge, and you've got an instant reminder of someone you love that can make you smile on a daily basis.

Take the time to turn a simple photo card into a special holiday greeting. Here are two easy options:

If your Christmas greeting list is long: Use an online photo site to create unique cards that you can personalize with a special note or decorative embellishment. Just choose the photo(s), upload them to the website (see Resources, page 124), and select a design for the card. You'll find every imaginable theme and variation in color, number, and arrangement of photos; background design elements; and greeting copy. A week later, you've got 50 to 500 photo cards in your mailbox, ready to write in and send out!

If your list is short (or you have more time): Get simple, nice quality, blank cards, then attach your photo using photo backing adhesive or photo corners (both available at most art supply stores). You can also find blank cards that already have four slots cut into the cover for a standard-size photo, or layered cards into which you can slide your image, which then shows through a "frame" cut out of the front.

Make a Holiday Stamp

kid friendly

A stamped card makes an artful and unique handmade greeting. The best part about using a stamp for Christmas cards is that you do the labor-intensive part just once—the rest is simple stamping.

You can choose to go with the elegance of a single image or a mash-up of multiple designs. Experiment with different colored inks, or add color with markers, pencils, or paints to get the design just as you imagined it.

Potato stamp: Cut a potato in half, draw or trace your design onto the flat surface, then carve out the outline with a paring knife or carving tool to cut around the image.

Simple foam stamp: Use a Christmas-themed cookie cutter to cut out a design from a piece of foam. You may need to use scissors to clean up the edges. Glue the foam onto a block of wood, and after it's dry, it's ready to be used as a stamp.

Lino-block stamp: You can take it up a notch and create your own linoleum-block stamp (which, by the way, can be reused—and for different purposes). Draw your design onto a piece of linoleum block, which can be purchased online or at any art supply store. From here, you can either carve out around the outline of the design, as with the potato stamp, or carve deeply into the block itself. Then, using either paint or an ink pad, press the design onto your card. Carving the outline will result in just the carved shape appearing on your card, while carving into the stamp will cover your entire card with color. You decide what look you want to achieve.

Those who can't imagine carving out a stamp of any type will be happy to know that every imaginable design is available at craft shops and online stamp purveyors. You'll find all manner of Christmas trees, angels, reindeer, snowmen, snowflakes, Santas, holly, bells, and much more.

Stitch Up a Greeting

Use simple needlework to make an exquisite and unique holiday card.

For those with even the most rudimentary sewing skills, making a hand-embroidered or machine-sewn card is a cool, crafty alternative to the standard holiday greeting. Think of the surprised smile of the recipient who opens this card.

All you need to get started is a blank card made out of heavy paper or cardstock, an embroidery needle, embroidery floss, and a little imagination.

1. Draw your design on the front of a blank card. A star is simple yet festive; if you're feeling artistic, try a snowman, reindeer, or the words "Merry Christmas!"

2. Choose the color of your embroidery floss and decide if you're going to use the same color on the entire design or different spots of color in different places.

3. Thread your embroidery needle with the floss. If you're a beginner, use a straight running stitch to begin sewing along the drawn lines: the simpler the stitch, the cleaner it will look. If you're confident of your stitching ability, try other stitches, such as whip stitch, stem stitch (page 85), chain stitch, or cross stitch. You may even want to have some French knots scattered across the card to look like tiny stars or snowflakes.

4. When you're done stitching, use tape to secure the end of the thread to the back of the card.

∗ For the more advanced sewer, slip the card underneath the sewing machine, and sew over your drawn design. Just make sure your needle is strong enough to sew on heavy paper or cardstock.

Don't be intimidated by the amount of time it'll take to make all of your cards. While keeping your hands busy with the embroidery, catch up on your favorite television series or listen to an audiobook.

Fashion a Felt Card

Felt is a fabulous choice for a holiday card—its warm texture, bold colors, and three-dimensionality are guaranteed to give any card project a tactile appeal.

Easy to use for all ages, felt is a versatile material that is inexpensive, cuts easily, does not fray or tatter, and adheres to cardstock or paper with liquid craft glue. Enhance an existing card design with felt or use a blank card to make an original work of art. Here are a few suggestions to get you started.

Geometric pieces card: Cut pieces of felt in basic geometric shapes and combine them into recognizable forms, such as a Christmas tree (one large triangle or three triangles of increasing size), ornaments (small circles), a house (triangle and square), presents (small squares and rectangles), a Santa hat (triangle and a circle), a snowman (three circles of increasing size), and holly (a long, thin rectangle and circles). Glue them to your card, and you're done. The possibilities are endless!

Simple reverse cut-out card: Draw animal shapes, stars, angels, or snowmen onto the felt; use a sharp blade to cut the figures out. Glue the felt outline to a card, and your design will be revealed in reverse.

Felt postcard: Cut out a piece of felt and a piece of cardboard, both in the size of a postcard—4¼ by 6 inches (10.5 x 15 cm). Glue them together and trim the edges so that they match. Create your design on the front, and write your holiday greeting on the back. Add a stamp and send it off in the mail as a postcard. (Do make sure the glue is dry and the felt and stamp are securely adhered to the cardboard.)

All of these ideas can also be applied to making ornaments. Just punch a hole at the top of your design and thread it with a pretty ribbon.

Reuse Paint Color Chips

Create unique cards that are also eco-friendly.

Next time you come home from the hardware store with a fistful of paint samples, consider using them for a different type of project: your Christmas cards. The progressively deepening hues of color make a beautiful backdrop or pattern that can be used a number of different ways. The variations are endless, so adapt these ideas as you see fit; the idea is to take advantage of the sturdy, colorful paper in clever ways.

* You can glue the entire piece onto blank cards and decorate each square, either with words ("Merry Christmas & Happy New Year!"), stickers, or, if you've got the time and inclination, cut and paste photos of you and your family, giving the card the appearance of a photo booth picture set.

* Cut the wider paint chip samples into triangular Christmas tree shapes, stars, and snowmen (three circles on top of each other), and then embellish with stickers, glitter, or shapes cut from other paint chips.

* If you're adept at drawing, sketch the silhouette of a tree branch and cardinal, or other Christmas icon.

You can also use paint chips as gift tags, garlands, nametags for place settings, or tree ornaments.

Construct a Pop-Up Card

Surprise your friends and family with a pop-up greeting.

A pop-up card lends itself well to any design you'd like to use: a snowman, a Christmas tree, a snowflake, a star, a dove—or words like "Noel" or "Peace." It's also a great way to showcase your favorite family photo.

To get started, you'll need either a blank folding card or an 8- by 10-inch (20 x 25 cm) piece of cardstock folded horizontally.

1. From the outside crease of the folded card, cut two short (about 1½ or 2 inch; 3.5 or 5 cm) parallel lines about ½ inch (1 cm) apart from each other, equidistant from the center of the card.

2. With your card open to an L shape, gently push in the slice you've just cut, so it pops forward (away from the crease). This will create the support for your image.

3. Cut a design (tree, star, snowflake, photo) from cardstock or heavy paper. Use a glue stick to apply glue to the pop-out support, then adhere your design to the backing and press the card closed so it dries securely.

> You can also use multiple images on the same card by cutting out two or three slots instead of one.

kid friendly

Collage a Card

Recycle magazines and catalogs to make cut-and-paste Christmas cards.

Magazine editors spend months finding and curating the perfect holiday images for home design, lifestyle, and fashion magazines, and even those mail-order catalogs that are heaped into your mailbox by the pound. Rather than tossing them into the recycling bin, why not use them to create your own pieces of original art?

Using standard scissors (or pinking shears, for a more decorative edge) cut out images that you like: Christmas trees, holly, candles, fire, snowy scenes, or anything that conveys the holiday spirit. Then decide on a visual theme to organize the images. Collect some blank cards, glue, and any embellishments (such as ribbon or glitter) you think would look nice, and you're ready to start. Here are some suggestions.

✳ Cut circles or onion shapes from the pages. Glue them on to the card and draw a line from the top of the shape to the top of the card to make them look like ornaments.

✳ Cut out a square from a glossy, colorful page and glue rickrack ribbon around its outside edges to make it look like a present.

✳ Cut out key words like "Celebrate" or "Noel" and paste them onto the card—try a vertical or diagonal orientation for a fresh look.

✳ If you find a page that's uniformly bright or deep in color with few images, use that as the backdrop for other images you can layer on top of it.

✳ Make a decoupage card. Cut out holiday shapes—simple trees, snowmen, or stars—and affix them to your card. You can opt for a very simple, elegant look, such as a single Christmas tree with a star at the top, or make it more elaborate, with multiple overlapping images. A sealer will keep the finish smooth.

✳ Hang a stocking. Poke two small holes, one at either side of the card, then string baker's twine in a swooping line across the top of the card. Glue the shape of a stocking you cut from a magazine to the line.

✳ With a hole punch, cut out little circles from silver- or golden-colored pages and use them as shining accents.

Magazine pages make an excellent source of paper for all kinds of holiday projects. Save them up all year, then pull out your stash as December nears and have some fun.

∗ Use single pages to wrap small presents.

∗ Tape or glue pages together to create a collage-style wrap for larger gifts.

∗ Cut out cardboard shapes and glue colorful pages to the front and back, then attach a hook or string to make ornaments.

∗ Fold and glue individual pages to make envelopes (find templates online). Last year's calendar is another good source of envelope paper.

> The key to achieving a polished look is restraint and appreciation for blank space. Rather than randomly gluing all types of images on the card, try sticking to a palette of two or three colors at most and one primary image with a smattering of embellishment.

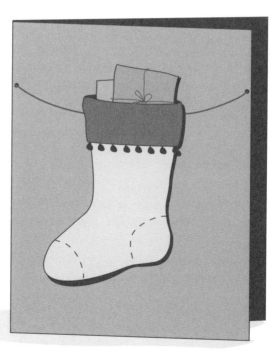

Recycle Cards of Christmases Past

Greetings come around again when you reuse this year's cards for next year's holiday décor.

Giving and receiving holiday cards is a thoughtful way to express your appreciation to those who are important to you. Here are a few creative ways to reuse and enjoy these cards once again—and it's much more satisfying than just placing them in the recycling bin!

Next year's cards: Some of the cards you receive will delight you, so why not transform and send them back out to please someone else? Find the images and designs you like best—perhaps an angel or a particularly cute Santa or Rudolph caught your eye—and cut them out. Once you go through all your cards, you'll end up with a pile of great images that can be remade into next year's Christmas cards. Glue the images onto plain cards now, so they're ready to go, or wait until inspiration hits you next Christmas. The Pop-Up Cards on page 19 and the Collage Cards on page 20 are also great ways to show off your favorite images.

Gift tags: No need to buy gift tags when they can be easily made from last year's cards. The sturdy cardstock is just the right weight for gift tags. Just make sure the back side of the card you cut is blank to leave space for filling in the name of your gift recipient.

Garland: Gather together your favorite Christmas cards from seasons past, and splay them over a ribbon. Or cut off the fronts of the cards, discarding the backs. Punch a small hole in one corner of each card front, then string and thread a piece of colorful ribbon through all the holes. Now drape your garland along a fireplace mantel, around the stairway banister, or around the Christmas tree. For a vertical garland, glue the cards in a straight line down a ribbon and hang alongside a doorway.

Advent calendar: Choose twenty-five of your favorite cards from years past and present, and detach the front of the card, recycling the rest of the card. On the back side of the image, decoratively write, stamp, or paint the day of the month. Hang all of the cards on baker's twine with clothespins or paper clips with the numbers facing forward. As you count down to the big day, turn the cards around to reveal their merry images.

Original artwork: If you admire a handmade card, honor the artist by framing the image. If it's holiday-themed, you can display it every Christmas as part of your holiday décor.

Place mats: This project is super-easy (great for new crafters or kids). Pile last year's cards on the table and start cutting away. Place the pieces together in different shapes and sizes, and use colored construction paper as a backing. Glue your pieces to the construction paper, and take it to the copy shop to be laminated. Now you'll have festive place mats to use every holiday season.

Bookmarks: Slice up your cards into long rectangles, punch a hole in their tops, and thread a ribbon through. Tie a knot and cut off any dangling ends. Keep these holiday bookmarks for your own use or slip one into a book you're giving as a gift. They're also nice decorations for the outside of a package that contains a book.

Recipe cards: Write down your favorite Christmas recipes on the blank back sides of cards, and keep them for your own use or to share with your friends and family.

Charitable reuse: The children's non-profit organization St. Jude's Ranch recycles Christmas cards into cards that are sold to raise funds for the program. Just send your cards to the following address:

St. Jude's Ranch for Children Recycled Card Program
100 St. Jude's Street
Boulder City, NV 89005

Go Hi-Tech

Send season's greetings in no time with these virtual solutions.

Homemade and hi-tech: Can they coexist? Yes! With just a little creativity, digital greetings can capture the spirit of Christmas. They may lack the tactile pleasure of a card, but virtual greetings can convey all the warmth and festivity you'd put into a handmade card. Virtual cards save paper and shrink your carbon footprint! And they let you reach out to many more people swifty and easily.

Email: The easiest way to send a virtual Christmas card is by email. Use a holiday color scheme for your text or add a festive background to make your message more attractive. Attach a family photo or a scan of your child's holiday drawing. Or create a digital drawing of a winter scene and have the entire family include their signatures. Then hit "Send."

> When sending an email message to multiple recipients, always remember to enter the email addresses into the Bcc (blind carbon copy) line. Your acquaintances will greatly appreciate that you respect their privacy.

Video: If you're up for a slightly more involved, Web-engineered virtual greeting, videotape yourself and/or your family singing a favorite Christmas carol, spreading peace and joy, or sharing family gossip. Most digital cameras have video-taking capabilities, so all you have to do is upload the video onto a website, like YouTube or Vimeo, and send the link to your family and friends. Also, most computers come equipped with simple video-editing programs, so don't be afraid to get creative and let your inner director thrive!

E-cards: Though not as personal, there are a number of clever greeting card websites that may appeal to your aesthetic and humor. Most sites are divided into categories: funny, cute, traditional, or religious. With a little research, you will find some amazingly

> Some possible drawbacks to sending e-cards are that your recipients will often be asked to register on the site before being allowed access to your greeting, and many email programs might tag these messages as spam.

elaborate holiday scenes complete with soundtracks. You will also find hilarious, highly polished videos of elves dancing (with options such as placing a picture of your head on a dancing elf's body), kittens singing, and chimps acting as St. Nick.

Blogs: If you don't already have a blog, now is a great time to start one. A blog lets people know what you're up to and, especially during Christmas, is a nice place to express your best wishes to all. Create-your-own-blog websites like WordPress, Blogger, and Tumblr make it easy to set up and maintain a blog just by registering with your email address. Write a blog post that lets friends and family know what you've been up to during the past year, share photos of projects or recipes you've made, upload some photos and videos, and give your recipients a view into your life. Just email your link when your blog is set up. If you want to keep your blog private, make sure to protect it with a password that you share only with friends and family.

Social Networking: Social networking websites like Facebook or MySpace are great for connecting with friends past and present. By convening all of your friends in one place on the Web, you can easily send a group holiday greeting or you can write individual notes. It's up to you!

Text or Tweet: If you've been too busy to put any effort into a holiday greeting, your last-ditch effort can be sending out a text message or a tweet (on Twitter) to your friends and family with the simple message, "Merry Christmas!"

chapter

TRIMMING

Light the candles, hang the garlands, decorate the tree with homemade ornaments. Let everyone know it's Christmas time!

By setting the stage for a festive holiday, you'll create a sense of excitement and anticipation for yourself, your family, and all those who come to visit. Dust off your box of ornaments and detangle last year's lights. Find your favorite ornaments and make new ones. Hang the wreaths and stockings. Display the holiday cards that have arrived in the mailbox. And, of course, trim the Christmas tree.

*

Decorating your home for Christmas is all about creating a mood with festive touches. You may have your favorite trimmings that you like to bring out each year, but it's also fun to craft new creations. Making and displaying holiday decorations with family members and friends will get everyone in the mood for celebration.

*

This chapter contains a wealth of tips and projects for homemade Christmas decorating, both inside and out. Creating a feeling of warm welcome can be as simple as switching off the electric lights in favor of candlelight or adding holiday trimmings around the house to create a festive feeling in every room.

*

Traditional crafts, like making wreaths and garlands, can suit any style, budget, and skill level. Try making a simple twig or pinecone wreath, or get the kids and grown-ups together to string popcorn garlands and fold wrapping paper chains for the tree. Those of you who have the time and inclination for more complex projects can make sophisticated wreaths and garlands with fresh and dried herbs, flowers, and berries, or whatever decorative elements suit your style.

✳

Included here are projects that can be displayed in every corner of the house—your own Advent calendar, opened daily to reveal a surprise, will heighten the anticipation; handmade snow globes add magic to a mantel or centerpiece; a row of handcrafted stockings will cheer up the staircase; a collection of delicate origami crane ornaments are a visual symbol of peace and hope. You'll also find suggestions for going green with your tree, specific projects to make for trimming the tree, and ideas for outdoor decorating, so you can bring the holiday cheer to the whole neighborhood.

✳

With all the festive decorations you make and display, your home is sure to convey feelings of warmth and merriment to all, and your homemade creations will become those you cherish the most, hold onto, and pass down from generation to generation.

Light the Candles

The evocative glow of candlelight creates a warm and festive ambience.

o fireplace? No problem! With a few cleverly arranged candles, it's easy to create the effect of a hearth in any room. Whether used solo to evoke a romantic glow or en masse for a lovely blaze, candles go a long way toward creating a homemade Christmas feeling—and using them may save on electricity, too.

Platter presentation: A cake platter makes a great pedestal for any object you want to show off, including a group of votives. Use votives that are the same size and color, such as short and white, or play with a palette of festive hues, like dark pinks and reds in varying heights. For additional sparkle, wrap the platter in foil. A shimmering collection of candles atop a platter makes a gorgeous centerpiece for a dining table, a kitchen counter, or a sideboard.

Ribbon bows: A simple gesture like tying a ribbon around a classic votive adds holiday flair. Choose vanilla- or cinnamon-scented candles, tie a neat bow around them, and place in groups or alone on a bedroom bureau, a bathroom counter, or a living room mantel. Mix plain-colored ribbons together (try chocolate brown with red, or bright green and white) for an easy two-toned effect.

Reflective sconce: If you have a mirrored sconce, place a candle in the holder to achieve dramatic effects. Or place candles on any flat mirror to create a sparkling display.

Warm welcome: Candlelight will give your entryway a glowing warmth perfect for greeting guests. A pillar candle in a large glass vase or hurricane jar, set on a hall table or a pair flanking your front door (inside or out), creates a welcoming mood.

Glittering candlelight: Maximize the glow with a little glitter! Pick out an elegant palette of two or three colors of glitter (e.g., gold, silver, and red, or two shades of soft pink paired with gold or silver), spray adhesive on the candles and roll them in the glitter. You can also try mixing the different colors of glitter together. Either way, the final look will be sparkly and fun.

Mantel drama: Place a series of votives—at least five—of the same height or varying heights in a line along a fireplace mantel, a shelf, or a picture rail. Try weaving a garland or pine tree branches around the candles for added embellishment (see Go For Garlands, page 38).

Fireplace yule log: A fireplace that doesn't function can still be used as it was originally intended—to host a radiant blaze. Simply place a dozen pillar candles in varying heights in the fireplace, cover with a grate (as a safety precaution), and let it glow. If you don't have a grate, place the candles in hurricane jars or large glass vases.

Pillar and snow: Create an outdoorsy Christmas centerpiece by placing three or four pillar candles on a plate with some fake snow, pine branches and pinecones, and a few dried cranberries for a dash of color.

Don't forget to take safety precautions when using candles, especially around children and pets. Keep them out of reach and have a fire extinguisher handy as a preventative measure.

No-drip candles can be expensive; fortunately, you can make tapered candles practically drip-proof with an overnight soak in saltwater. In a plastic container wide enough to hold the candles, dissolve $1/3$ cup (100 g) salt in 2 cups (475 ml) warm water. Add the candles, place a can or other weight on top of the candles to keep them submerged, and soak overnight. Let the candles dry completely before using.

kid friendly

Make a Stocking

"The stockings were hung by the chimney with care . . ."
— from "The Night Before Christmas"

Making a homemade stocking is easy, even for a non-crafter. Try one of these simple stockings. This is a great project for children; younger kids will need some help while older children can be set up with the materials and left alone to create their own stocking masterpieces.

CLASSIC FELT STOCKING

1. Felt can be found at any craft store, and it comes in a wealth of colors. Choose one you like, and purchase more than you think you'll need.

2. Create a template or pattern of a stocking.

3. Trace the template or pin it to the felt, and cut two pieces.

4. Line the pieces up and either sew (a whipstitch is easy and decorative), or glue the edges of the two pieces together with fabric glue.

5. Embellish with more felt, ribbons, beads, buttons, patches, or glitter. Add a name to personalize it.

> Felt isn't the only fabric that is great for a stocking. Any fabric that can be sewn can be turned into a lovely sock. Just turn the two cut-out pieces of fabric inside out and sew the pieces together with a sewing machine or with a very secure hand stitch. Then, hem the edge of the open top. Turn your stocking right side out, and it's ready to go.

SWEATER SLEEVE STOCKING

1. Choose a sweater that you don't wear anymore and cut off the sleeve.

2. Sew one end of the sleeve together securely, so it can hold all of the goodies.

3. Pick out a contrasting or complementary yarn and whipstitch a decorative edge that will also prevent any unraveling.

4. Embellish as you wish.

Hang an Alternative Stocking

In lieu of the classic felt or knit stocking, try mixing it up with these fun alternatives.

Refresh the tradition of the Christmas stocking by choosing an unconventional container for your stocking stuffers. You might be inspired by different cultural traditions, decorating themes, or personal enthusiasms. Just as you would a traditional stocking, hang them from the mantel, a stairway, window ledge, or doorframe; or place them on a side table.

Red silk slippers: This exotic option can be found in most Chinatown shops or on the Internet. Simply sew a loop around the heel end of the slipper, hang it with a ribbon or some twine, and fill with goodies.

Striped athletic socks: For the sporty family, here's a clever substitute. Choose white socks with red or green stripes to match the holiday décor.

Oven mitts: Perfect for any cooking enthusiast, an oven mitt is sturdy, colorful, and roomy enough to hold a lot of Christmas loot. The large thumb slot is also a great place to hide that small yet special gift.

Christmas tights: Red-and-white striped tights will look especially cute when the feet are filled with bulging goodies. Children's sizes should have plenty of room for stretch.

Rubber boots: Most colorful galoshes have hooks at the top, so they should be easy enough to hang. Just don't feel pressured to fill the entire boot with treats!

Clogs: It is believed that the Dutch actually started the "stocking" tradition by leaving their clogs—stuffed with carrots and straw for the reindeer—by the hearth for Santa Claus to fill with treats. Why not go Dutch and set out clogs?

Decorate with Leaves and Branches

Let nature decorate your home during the holidays with leaves and branches.

The sculptured shapes of bare branches, artfully arranged in your home, can make a stunning display. Leafy evergreen boughs bring the outdoors in—and smell delightful.

Miniature trees: Sculptural branches that look like miniature trees (with plenty of offshoots where ornaments can hang) can be found on the ground in your yard or at the local park. Once you find the perfect branch, pluck off any residual leaf matter, then place it in a vase that will hold its weight (no water necessary, of course). Try spray painting the branch white for a more elegant look. You can leave it bare, and enjoy the shape as is, or decorate with ornaments.

Pine: The aroma of pine boughs immediately evokes Christmas. Drape full branches across your fireplace mantel, bedroom bureau, or kitchen counter au naturel, or fancy them up with little red and silver ball ornaments.

Holly and Mistletoe*: Symbolic of everlasting life (along with ivy which all stay green throughout the winter), holly and mistletoe are holiday favorites. The sharply scalloped edges and bright red berries of holly branches make them ideal for display. Use florists' wire, which is readily found at craft and hobby stores, to make an arrangement (a posy or spray). Hang mistletoe from a well-placed doorway, with a long red or silver ribbon to make it noticeable.

Incorporating brightly colored fruit into the décor is many an interior designer's secret weapon. Fill a deep, clear vase with oranges or apples and use it as a natural centerpiece. Or nestle winter fruits like oranges, clementines, and pears among pine boughs for cheerful pops of color.

*Holly and mistletoe can be toxic if ingested, so make sure to keep out of reach of children and pets, or choose a non-toxic alternative.

Weave a Wreath

Symbolic of the circle of life, wreaths are welcoming and festive.

You can be creative with the type of wreath you want to make, and where you want to hang it. Hang one on your front door, on an interior door, in a big picture window, from a staircase, or on a fence in your yard. Table wreaths can be centerpieces, candle surrounds, or simply ornamental.

Start with a base, readily available at craft stores in styles from natural (grapevine or willow) to manufactured (wire or foam), or make it yourself. Then affix your wreath materials using florists' wire, hot glue, or twine.

Greens: Pine boughs, eucalyptus, bay leaves, ivy—the smell of fresh boughs or herbs will waft through the house when you hang a fresh green wreath. You can also add a few carefully placed white or silver ornaments.

Dried: Dried flower or foliage wreaths have a vintage feeling that is especially charming over the holidays. Choose "everlasting" blooms or leaves that keep their color when dried—whether roses from your own garden or classic stems, such as yarrow, that you can find at craft stores. For an especially rustic feel, try incorporating some raffia leaves.

Personalized: Wreath embellishments are limited only by your imagination, so why not make a wreath that reflects your personal interests or style? Any object, multiplied by two dozen or more and attachable to a circular frame, can be used to make a wreath. Possible wreath materials include peacock feathers, Christmas lights, extension cords, ball ornaments, beads, gumdrops, buttons, crocheted doilies, paper leaves, silver-sprayed zip ties, small pieces of driftwood, tiny wrapped gifts, soaps, and even Barbie dolls!

Miniature: Using twigs from your own yard, construct mini wreaths to encircle candles. Or attach a ribbon loop and hang them from doorknobs.

Even the simplest of wreaths can be enhanced with taffeta, velvet, or silk ribbon tied in a large, lovely bow. If your bow-tying skills are lacking, just take your chosen ribbon to the local florist—make sure there is plenty of ribbon for the florist to work with. For a minimal fee, the florist will tie a beautiful bow for you and add wire to the back so it can easily attach to your wreath.

Grow a Holiday Plant

Bring your home to life with winter blooms.

resh-cut flowers are beautiful, but ephemeral—a Christmas plant, however, will keep on blooming through the season and beyond. Pot one of these traditional winter-blooming plants in a fetching container; keep it watered and happy during the year, and you'll be rewarded with beautiful blooms that flower just in time for the holidays. Plant it outdoors after the holiday season is over and watch it thrive in your yard.

Poinsettia*: The quintessential Christmas plant can be found everywhere during the holidays. Rather than leaving the plant in the plastic pot it comes in and disposing of it once the holidays have passed, repot it in a container you value and let it live. Though the poinsettia will eventually lose its leaves, if you nurture it—water only when the soil is dry, keep it at normal room temperature, and place out of direct sunlight—the brightly colored leaves will return in late November next year. To ensure the colorful leaves come back, here's a gardener's secret: Place the plant in total darkness for at least fourteen hours a day, starting around the first of October (a dark closet at night works well). During the day, it should see the light of day for at least six hours, and by Christmas, the new growth should show the blush of the season.

Cyclamen: The delicate red, pink, or white blooms and the marbled leaves of these plants will brighten any room. Cyclamen can bloom for up to four months if they're treated well. Make sure to keep the soil moist and the plant at room temperature. When the plant goes dormant during the summer months (its leaves will turn yellow), place it in a cool, dark place and allow the soil to dry out. Repot and start watering in September to encourage holiday blooms.

Freesia: These tall, fragrant flowers give off a lovely scent for the entirety of their bloom and come in a variety of colors, including red and white. To care for freesia, keep the soil well-drained and the plant near full sunlight, if possible. It also thrives in cool nighttime temperatures of 40°F to 45°F (4°C to 7°C). After the flowers are past bloom, save the corms to be planted outside in the spring.

Narcissus: The white wintertime variety of this genus, also known as paperwhite, is telltale sign of the season. You'll never mistake its sharp and tangy fragrance. When placed around the house in decorative pots, the lithe, lengthy stalks will command attention. Very easy to grow, the bulbs can be planted late in the season, and with proper watering, you'll have blooms within four weeks. What's more, paperwhites do not require soil; pebbles or glass marbles work just as well and are more decorative.

Christmas cactus: These plants look like typical succulents throughout the year, but come the holidays, they explode into dramatic pink or yellow blooms. The brighter the light they receive, the deeper the color of the flowers, but if the sunlight is too intense, the leaves will burn. Keep the soil well-drained and water the plant thoroughly when the soil becomes dry. Next October, stop watering the plant altogether, and then begin watering again very lightly in November, making sure the leaves don't become too bloated and droopy. Keep it in temperatures between 55°F (13°C) at night and 65°F (18°C) during the day, and you're guaranteed to see those lovely blossoms for Christmas.

Amaryllis: An increasingly popular holiday gift, these leggy beauties are grown from bulbs and can be found in most garden shops. They will flower for at least seven and up to ten weeks if they're kept at around 68°F (20°C) in a brightly lit spot—but not in direct sunlight—and watered well. After the plant has flowered, you can make it bloom again by cutting the flower to just a couple of inches above the bulb.

*Poinsettia can be toxic if ingested, so make sure to keep your plant out of reach of children and pets, or choose a plant that is non-toxic.

Go for Garlands

Festoon your home with colorful garlands for a celebratory feel.

Super easy and versatile, garlands add flourish to your home. Ideal for a tree, garlands also look festive hanging across mantels, doorways, and window frames; they can be hung vertically from a doorframe or molding or be draped across a table or bureau.

Ribbon or paper loops: Kids love to help make these fun garlands. Cut 1- by 6-inch (2.5 x 15 cm) pieces of fancy ribbon, holiday paper, or construction paper, make a loop, and fasten the ends together with glue or tape. Loop the next strip through and fasten. Repeat the step and keep adding ribbon or paper loops until your garland reaches the desired length.

Dried pasta: Another great project for kids is the decorating and stringing of dried pasta. Buy a variety of pasta shapes that are tubular like elbow macaroni, rigatoni, penne, ziti, and ruote, (aka, wagon wheels)—for simple stringing. Next, decide on a pattern for your garland, unless you prefer a random order. Before stringing the pasta, have the kids color each piece using markers, or for a more elegant look, spray-paint each piece silver or gold.

> Hang your garlands from unexpected spots—chandeliers, bookshelves, mirrors, lampshades, paintings, curtain rails, headboards, a bedroom bureau, kitchen pot rack, or the backs of dining room chairs.

Popcorn and dried cranberries: Using a regular sewing needle and strong, nylon thread, string the pieces together one by one. Alternate one kernel of popcorn with one cranberry, or string five kernels of popcorn for every one cranberry. Experiment to achieve the look you want.

Greenery: Pine branches, holly, bay leaves, mistletoe—just about any winter greenery can be formed into a garland using twine, ribbon, or wire.

Large beads or pearls: String metallic beads and pearls together, then hang them in front of windows, where they will sparkle beautifully in the sunlight, or from the tree, where they can reflect the glow of lamps, candlelight, and Christmas lights.

Paper cutouts: Ask the kids to help you make paper cutouts of Christmas icons like snowmen, angels, and snowflakes, and string together vertically or horizontally with a festive ribbon.

Christmas lights: Hang strings of little white lights or old-fashioned, multicolored lights in arcs from your windows or ceilings.

Gingerbread garland: It doesn't matter if the cookies are homemade or store-bought. Once they're connected with pretty red ribbon or baker's twine and hung across the kitchen doorway, they make a room more cheery.

Ball ornaments: Tie a few sturdy ornaments together with twine and attach the bouquet to a long piece of heavy yarn or rope. In lieu of a wreath, hang this from a nail or hook on your front door.

Fabric or felt banner: Put all those remnants of fabrics you've been holding on to— you just didn't know exactly why—to creative use. Cut them into triangular shapes, attach them to heavy thread or baker's twine, and hang them festively from the ceiling.

Decorative trim: A sewing or fabric store is a great place to find colorful, textured trim, which can be purchased by the yard or meter. Braiding, cording, tassels, sequins, lace, pom-pom fringe, rickrack, and patterned jacquard make instant garlands.

Make a Snow Globe

Capture a winter wonderland.

his simple snow globe project guarantees a white Christmas (no shoveling required!) no matter where you live. Shake it up and watch your miniature world come to life in a tiny snow shower.

1. Choose miniatures (e.g., houses, trees, deer, elves, or Santa) made of plastic, rubber, glass, or ceramic that can be purchased at a toy store, a specialty dollhouse shop, or online.

2. Pick out a clear glass jar with a lid from your recycling bin.

3. Use a strong, waterproof glue to affix your miniatures to the inside of the lid of the jar. The lid is going to act as the base of your snow globe.

4. Fill the jar with water and a good dose of glitter or fake snow, which can be purchased at a craft store.

5. When the glue has dried on the jar lid with your miniatures securely attached, carefully place the lid onto the top of the jar and screw it on tightly.

6. Glue around the edge of the lid to make sure it's completely sealed from leaks.

7. Place your snow globe on your mantel or tabletop, and give it a shake whenever you want a little sparkle.

For an all-natural snow substitute, thoroughly clean and lightly crumble eggshells.

Craft an Advent Calendar

Counting down to the big day is almost as exciting as waking up on Christmas morning.

An Advent calendar adds to the excitement of the holidays, especially for kids, by marking off each day until Christmas with a little surprise. Even a simple calendar can hold seasonal messages, clever jokes, or individually wrapped treats.

Paper envelopes: Find pretty paper envelopes and write or stamp the day of the month at the bottom. Hang a line of baker's twine and attach the envelopes with colorful paper clips or clothespins. Or punch a hole (with a hole punch) in the corner of each envelope and attach the group to a ring.

Miniature stockings: Stuff little socks with small surprises; they will look adorable hanging from a red ribbon with each one uniquely decorated with beads, glitter, or felt cutouts.

Little gift boxes or matchboxes: Here's your chance to put those little boxes you've accumulated to good use. Wrap each one as if it were a little package.

Mittens and socks: All those mismatched mittens and socks can finally be appropriated for a good cause. Fasten them to a line of twine with clothespins.

Tins: Little tins that originally held mints or chocolates can add up to a cool and crafty advent calendar. Once you've accumulated twenty-five of them, glue them to a white poster board or add magnets to the back and place on the refrigerator. Then write the numbers directly on the lids or on labels that you can affix to the lids.

> If you've got the time and the disposition, use an Advent calendar for organizing your holiday activities and tasks as they correspond to each day of the month (e.g., decorate the tree, make a wreath, donate food to a shelter, start making gifts, wrap gifts, throw a Christmas party, and so on).

Get an Earth-Friendly Christmas Tree

All the information you need to make the most green decision about your Christmas tree.

Every holiday season, most of us face a Christmas tree conundrum: Is it better for the environment to have a real or an artificial tree? It can be a complicated question, but there are ways to have your Christmas tree and enjoy it, too!

REAL TREES

A real tree is the best option for the environment, if you are sure to choose carefully. Make sure that the tree you are buying is locally grown, so there is less fuel used to transport it to a tree lot near you. Try to find an organically grown tree. Christmas tree farms add oxygen to the atmosphere and remove carbon dioxide. Many tree farms also stick to sustainable business models and plant multiple trees for every one they cut down and sell. Here are some more eco-conscious tips to help you have a green Christmas.

Look for a potted, living tree: Once Christmas has passed, keep your living tree outside in its container until the spring, when you can plant it in your yard (these trees usually come with a card that explains how to replant and care for them). The tree will reward you with its longevity.

Rent a tree: A number of communities are beginning to offer services that let you adopt a potted tree for the holidays, that is later picked up from your home and planted elsewhere.

Recycle your tree: Most urban communities offer a tree recycling service, picking up the tree on particular trash days and turning it into mulch. If your city does not offer this service, you may be able to find a nearby facility that does.

Reuse your tree: Use the stripped tree as a trellis in the garden for planting vines, or place the aromatic branches in little muslin bags as potpourri for your linen drawers.

ARTIFICIAL TREES

An argument can be made that artificial trees are great for their longevity and use year after year; unfortunately, they are non-biodegradable and made of plastic that may contain toxins. They also leave a larger carbon footprint, as they are mostly manufactured overseas and must be shipped.

If you prefer an artificial tree or already own one, here are some helpful tips to make as little impact on the environment as possible.

Buy secondhand: Scout out thrift stores, flea markets, and online auction websites for gently used trees. Aluminum trees from the 1950s have a retro-modern and fun feeling.

Take extra good care of your tree: Try to keep your tree in great shape so it can be used for many years to come. If there is any wear and tear, do your best to camouflage it with lovely decoration.

Reuse or donate your tree: Whatever you do, try not to throw your tree away. If your tree is looking incredibly shabby, at the very least save the boughs that are intact and redeploy them as decoration around the house. If you have a tree that is still in good condition, donate it to a school, church, community center, or thrift shop.

TREE ALTERNATIVES

If you are still undecided, here are some non-traditional alternatives.

Indoor plant or tree: Decorate other types of plants or trees you may already have in your home. Norfolk pine plants look just like Christmas trees when adorned with a few ornaments.

Ladder: The triangular shape of a ladder lends itself as a creative option. Show your arty, clever side by wrapping it with lights and adorning with a few special ornaments.

Boxes: Arrange a variety of beautifully wrapped boxes in the shape of a tree, with the biggest box on the bottom, going all the way to the smallest box on top.

Host a Make-Your-Own-Ornament Party

kid friendly

Handcrafted ornaments have meaning that a manufactured item can't match.

Made with love and hung with care, the homemade ornament captures the spirit of tree trimming. Gather family and friends early in the season to make a few simple ornaments together. Provide the materials and some good cheer, and you've got the makings for an unforgettable occasion. Here's how to throw an ornament party with festive projects that everyone can enjoy.

* Assemble materials in advance. Make sure there are tools and materials for everyone. Get several bottles of tacky glue, a few pairs of scissors (including safety scissors if kids are coming), and enough crafting supplies so everyone can work together. You may want to precut paper or fabric shapes to make it super easy.

* Show pictures or examples of finished ornaments so everyone knows what they're making.

* Gather around a big table or sit on the floor and get started.

Recycled wrapping paper chain: If you ever made gum wrapper chains, this project will seem familiar. School-age children will enjoy this project, too. Gather lots of old wrapping paper scraps. (If you want, organize them by color.) Cut them into rectangles approximately 1 by 3 inches (2.5 x 7.5 cm).

1. Fold one piece in half the long way, then unfold.

2. Fold each edge into the center. Then fold in half again.

3. Now fold the two short edges together so it makes a V shape.

4. Fold the short edges into the center of the V. That's one link.

5. Once you have made lots of links, you can start making your chain. Slide the first link's ends through the second link's loops.

6. Repeat until your chain is as long you'd like.

Felt presents: These sweet, little ornaments are easy for everyone to make, including young children and non-crafty grown-ups. You'll need several bottles of tacky glue, scissors (or you can pre-cut the shapes and have them ready), numerous pieces of colored felt, and a couple yards or meters of colored yarn for hanging loops.

1. Cut a rectangle approximately 2 by 3 inches (5 x 7.5 cm) from a piece of felt.

2. Cut two "ribbon" strips from a different color of felt, each about ⅛ inch (20 mm) wide. Make one long enough to cover the rectangle from top to bottom, and the other to cross its width.

3. Glue the strips to the rectangle in a cross shape.

4. Fold the yarn in half to make a loop and glue to the back of the present.

5. Let dry completely before hanging.

Silver and gold walnuts: Evoke eras past with these little ornaments. (This project is probably best suited for teens and grown-ups.) You will need empty walnut shells, gold and silver craft paint, paint brushes, tacky glue, and colored ribbon or yarn for a hanging loop.

1. Paint each half of the shell either gold or silver. Let dry.

2. Glue a thin strip along the inner edge of each shell.

3. Fold your hanging loop and place it between the shells. Press the glue-covered edges together, being sure to catch the loop. Let dry completely before hanging.

> More Christmas crafting gatherings you might host.
> • **Embellish-the-linens party:** Embroidery, fabric painting, and appliqué are just a few ways to add Christmas motifs to tea towels, pillowcases, hand towels, oven mitts, and other linens.
> • **Christmas crockery:** Ceramics and glass of all sorts can be painted (on the outside, please) to make Christmas dessert plates, votive holders, and candy dishes.

Fold an Origami Ornament

A symbol of peace, the crane is a wonderful Christmas ornament to make and give.

Origami, the traditional Japanese art of folding paper, lends itself perfectly to ornament making. These paper silhouettes capture the essence of any number of forms, from a crane to a star. Once you get started on this addictive craft, you may find yourself folding an entire tree's worth of different origami ornaments. Origami paper comes in a range of colors, as well as beautiful patterns; but simple craft paper will yield an equally striking ornament.

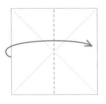

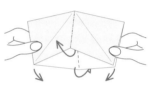

1. Choose a square piece of paper with a nice color or pattern on one side. With the colored side facing you, fold in half, then open. Fold in half the other way and open.

2. Turn the paper to the other side; repeat Step 1 so that you have 4 sharp creases.

3. Holding the short sides, fold the top 3 corners together to collapse the model as shown.

closed end

cut edges   cut edges

4. Bring the left side flaps together and repeat on the right. Flatten.

5. Fold the front side flaps into the center as shown. Crease well and unfold.

6. Fold the top triangle down as shown, then crease well.

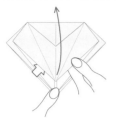 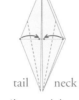 

wings

tail   neck

7. Open the top flap while pressing the sides of the model inwards until the long side edges meet at the center. Flatten.

8. Turn the model over and repeat Steps 5 through 7 on the other side. Flatten and smooth.

9. Fold the lower side edges inward toward the center (front layer only).

neck

wing

tail

10. Turn over and repeat on the other side.

11. Fold up 1 long point as high as it will go, and crease firmly. Repeat with the other point.

12. Holding as shown, inside-reverse fold the right point (this is the crane's neck) up between the wings. Repeat on the other side (this is the crane's tail).

13. Gently tug the crane's neck forward. Repeat with its tail. Pinch the bottom edges to firmly hold the new position.

14. Inside-reverse fold the top end of the neck to make the crane's head.

15. Fold down the wings. Now you have a beautiful crane ornament! Add a hanging loop (thread a needle and make a loop through the crane's back) or simply set atop a branch or table.

Dazzle Your Neighbors

Spread holiday cheer through the neighborhood with outdoor holiday displays.

Decorating the outside of your home and your yard publicly proclaims your love of the holidays. Whether your style is understated or over-the-top, there are lots of homemade decorations you can use to give your home some holiday curb appeal.

Decorate the door: The front door—typically your main entrance and usually visible from the street—is a perfect place to start.

∗ Place a traditional wreath made of greens, pinecones, twigs, or dried flowers on the door.

∗ Cover the entire door in gift wrap, or make a "ribbon" from two perpendicular strips of paper. Keep it green by using plain kraft paper (old paper bags unfolded will do) decorated by the kids, recycled gift wrap from years past, or fabric scraps.

∗ Make a holiday banner using colored felt and place at eye level.

∗ Drape a garland across the top and down the sides of the door frame; if you have a door knocker, trail colored ribbons from it.

Make the entry welcoming: The path leading up to your door and the area around the doorway itself are prime Christmas decorating spots.

∗ A symbol of the season, light is always welcoming. Add a warm glow with luminaries, which can be used to line a path or to flank the doorway. You can make them from old jam jars (clean, decorate as you like, and pop a votive in each); paper bags (cover the bottom with kitty litter or sand, and place a candle or battery-powered votive inside); or tin cans (remove the label, punch holes with an awl, and add a candle).

* Transform your year-round planters, window boxes, or birdbaths with lights, tinsel, or other trimmings.

Adorn your windows: The warm glow of a lit window at night is a longstanding symbol of welcome. Take it up a notch with these ideas.

* Place a single electric candle in each front-facing window for a simple but spectacular look.

* Let the kids create "stained-glass" windows with special window paint (available at craft stores).

* Hang small wreaths so that they dangle in front of windows—the light from indoors will frame them prettily.

Light up the neighborhood: Go earth-friendly with your light show by replacing older incandescent light strands (when they wear out) with new, energy-efficient LED lights or solar lights. Smaller bulbs, timers set for a specific period, and blinking lights can also help you save on electricity use.

* Design a light show that reflects your style—choose a theme that is meaningful to you, whether it is a simple row of white lights around the doorframe or a multicolored Christmas scene.

* Choose a color scheme for your lights—a single color or a combination of two colors is at once simple and dramatic.

* If you're more ambitious, try depicting a Christmas symbol or scene (the outline of a Christmas tree, a group of twig reindeer draped in twinkling lights, or a crèche scene lit all around).

* If you love the look of a brightly lit holiday extravaganza, go all-out with an exuberant light show covering all available surfaces.

chapter

COOKING

Bring family and friends together to celebrate while enjoying irresistible homemade dishes.

easting is an essential part of celebrating Christmas. As the holidays approach, and plans are made for gathering loved ones, food is invariably at the heart of it all. Special meals, baked goods, and treats prepared with love create mouth-watering aromas that emanate from the kitchen. And the kitchen is where most people gravitate, especially this time of year, whether they want to catch up on the latest news over snacks, to pitch in and help prepare meals, or to have a cozy chat with the cook.

﹡

Whether you're looking forward to preparing a sumptuous Christmas day feast from scratch or trying to find time to make your annual batch of cookies to share with your colleagues (or kids), this chapter offers homemade cooking ideas for every scenario. You'll be armed with recipes that will please the gamut of guests, from picky eaters to sophisticated gourmands.

﹡

As the season approaches, you'll want to get ready by stocking your pantry with lots of tasty snacks. Here you'll find suggestions for basics to keep on hand, so it's easy to whip together a quick plate of refreshments or a simple meal to enjoy with company. Also included are suggestions for hearty family meals you can prepare swiftly and enjoy more than once.

*

A holiday party is a perfect way to extend Christmas greetings and show appreciation for friends and neighbors; by inviting guests into your home to celebrate together, you embody the meaning of the season. Here, we provide recipes for homemade hors d'oeuvres, mulled wine, and Christmas punch.

*

Baked goods are wonderful treats to have on hand and make much-appreciated gifts. In this chapter you'll find ideas for sweets of all sorts, from cookies to quick breads to candy. Try a recipe for pumpkin bread, and send a few loaves to the neighbors. Candied orange peels make for a sophisticated sweet. And, don't forget cookies. Kids of all ages will be delighted to help, so why not organize a cookie-decorating party?

*

Small gifts of food make thoughtful presents that are always appreciated. Try making homemade preserves, an old-fashioned holiday tradition that you can easily adapt. Here you'll find easy recipes for spicy-sweet chutney and berry jam that you can make in winter. These recipes might even find a place on your own table if you plan to host the main event. And to offer some inspiration, we present a selection of Christmas day menus, including traditional Christmas dinners, vegetarian options, and even a Christmas brunch.

*

Have a delicious homemade Christmas!

Stock the Pantry

'Tis the season for visits, so stock your pantry with special offerings that will tempt all palates.

Keep easy and delicious snacks on hand for houseguests, relatives, friends, neighbors, and your own brood. It's a good idea to have some extra nonperishables available for noshing, and rotate the more delicate food items as befits the mood. Pack your cupboards with the ingredients necessary to make your favorite festive treats to share.

THE HOLIDAY PANTRY LIST

* Breads and crackers are essentials, so stock up!

* If you want to be able to whip together a satisfying spontaneous cheese plate, have on hand one each of a soft and mild variety (such as chèvre or brie); a soft and pungent (try taleggio or pont l'eveque); a firm and mild type (manchego, gouda); and a semi-soft and strong-flavored cheese (sharp cheddar, Danish blue).

* Olives of every type are excellent finger foods you can store.

* Dried and smoked meats make simple yet substantial fare: Choose high-quality salami, prosciutto, sausage, or salmon to have on hand.

* A bowl of nuts makes a healthy and easy snack: Keep pistachios, almonds, cashews, or honey-roasted peanuts in stock. Better yet, opt for some walnuts or brazil nuts in the shell and break out your Christmas nutcracker and a silver bowl!

* Crudités will ensure everyone gets their vegetables: Make sure the fridge holds fresh carrots, celery, red and green peppers, broccoli, or cauliflower.

* Even a simple dip dresses up the vegetables—sour cream and dill, yogurt cucumber, hummus, spinach, artichoke, or black bean. Find simple recipes on the Web.

* Cheese spreads are fun and will keep in your fridge for a week: feta, goat cheese (see recipes on pages 68–69).

Bake a Loaf (or Two)

Since you can whip them up in a jiffy, why not make more than one at a time? Keep one and give the other!

Versatile enough to be served for breakfast, an afternoon snack, or dessert, a baked loaf or quick bread is a delicious holiday staple. Sweet or savory will work: Think pumpkin, zucchini, carrot, cranberry, cinammon, or banana bread. Pop a batch in the oven, and enjoy the wonderful aroma wafting through your home.

QUICK PUMPKIN BREAD* (makes 2 loaves; you'll need 2 loaf pans)

3½ cups (420 g) all-purpose flour

2½ cups (500 g) sugar

2 teaspoons (10 ml) salt

4 teaspoons (20 ml) baking powder

1 teaspoon (5 ml) cinnamon

½ teaspoon (2.5 ml) nutmeg

¼ teaspoon (1.25 ml) clove

2 cups (490 g) canned pumpkin puree

⅔ cup (160 ml) canola or vegetable oil

½ cup (120 ml) water

4 eggs

pecan halves

> See page 79 for great ideas on presenting food gifts.

1. Combine flour, sugar, salt, baking powder, and spices in a bowl.

2. In a separate bowl, mix together the pumpkin, oil, water, and eggs, and whisk by hand until thoroughly blended.

3. Add the dry ingredients to the bowl of wet ingredients and combine until the mixture is completely moistened and without lumps.

4. Pour the batter into 2 buttered loaf pans. Top with raw pecan halves, if desired.

5. Bake at 350°F (175°C) for 40 minutes until a toothpick comes out clean. Bake longer if it doesn't.

*Recipe by Heather Coppersmith

Make Sweet and Spicy Holiday Preserves

The old-fashioned homemade goodness of preserves makes for a great gift for everyone.

A homemade Christmas calls for preserves; whether it's the sweet flavor of the summer's ripe berries or the spicier thrill of chutney, you'll be glad you preserved the bounty of the season—and so will those who receive a nicely wrapped jar. If you're new to preserving, you'll want to prepare carefully; and even if preserving is a longstanding tradition in your home, please be sure to use the proper equipment and safe techniques.

APPLE AND RAISIN CHUTNEY*
(makes about 4 to 6 cups or 2 to 3 pints; you'll need hot, sterlized jars)

This easy and delectable chutney makes a delicious accompaniment to meat or cheese dishes.

4 pounds (1.8 kg) cooking apples, peeled, cored, and chopped (use a variety of apples)

4 medium-sized onions, peeled and finely chopped

2 cloves garlic, crushed

Juice of 1 lemon

1 tablespoon (15 ml) mustard seeds

3¾ cups (890 ml) cider vinegar

2⅔ cups (440 g) raisins (mix in golden raisins for variety)

1 tablespoon (15 ml) ground ginger

2 teaspoons (10 ml) salt

5⅓ cups (960 g) brown sugar

1. Place the apples, onions, garlic, lemon juice, mustard seeds, and 2½ cups (590 ml) vinegar in a large pan.

2. Bring to a boil, then reduce heat and simmer for 1 hour or until the mixture is soft, stirring occasionally to make sure the mixture doesn't stick to the bottom of the pan.

3. Add the raisins, ground ginger, salt, sugar, and remaining 1¼ cups (300 ml) vinegar, and simmer, stirring frequently, until the chutney is thick.

4. Ladle the mixture into hot canning jars, leaving about ¼-inch (5 mm) space, then cover with prepared lids, seal, and label. Store for 6 to 8 weeks before gifting to enhance flavors.

*Recipe by Diane Hiatt

MEMORIES OF SUMMER BERRY JAM
(makes 7 cups or 3½ pints; you'll need hot, sterilized jars)

If you didn't have time to preserve summer's raspberries, blueberries, and strawberries, don't despair—you can make a delicious berry jam with frozen berries, and your guests will be just as happy when they taste it.

1½ pounds (700 g) frozen mixed berries, thawed
2 teaspoons (10 ml) lemon rind, finely grated
1 tablespoon (15 ml) lemon juice
1¾ ounces (1 package or 49 g) powdered pectin
4½ cups (900 g) granulated sugar

1. In a large, heavy pot, thaw and mash the berries. Add lemon rind and juice; stir.

2. In a large mixing bowl, stir pectin with ¼ cup (50 g) sugar. Stir into berries, then bring mixture to a full rolling boil over high heat, stirring constantly.

3. Add remaining sugar, stirring till dissolved. Return to full boil, stirring constantly, for a full minute. Remove from heat.

4. Stir for 5 minutes, skimming off any foam. Ladle into hot canning jars, leaving about ¼-inch (5 mm) space. Cover with prepared lids. Boil in boiling water canner for 10 minutes. Let jars stand on rack until cool.

See page 79 for great ideas on presenting jars. Be sure to label, note the date it was made, and recommend some dishes for which this preserve would make a tasty accompaniment.

Bake Christmas Cookies

Christmas just wouldn't be Christmas without an array of festive cookies to offer to family and friends.

Cookies are holiday all-stars. Whether they're decorated, cut-out, bar, roll, drop, or sandwich, from your grandmother's recipe or a first-time experiment, Christmas cookies are as fun to make as they are to eat. Make big batches so you'll have plenty to serve, give away, and enjoy at home!

SHORTBREAD SUGAR COOKIES* (makes 40 cookies)

This classic holiday cookie tastes great, is easy to make, and is fun to decorate.

1½ cups (3 sticks, 340 g) butter softened to room temperature
¾ cup (150 g) granulated sugar
1½ teaspoons (7 ml) vanilla
3 cups (360 g) all-purpose flour
¾ teaspoon (3.75 ml) salt

1. Cream the butter, sugar, and vanilla until they're soft, then stir in the flour and salt until the dough forms. Shape into a ball.

2. Place the ball of dough on a floured surface and roll out with a floured rolling pin until it's ¼ inch (5 mm) thick.

3. Use festive cookie cutters to cut the dough into your favorite shapes.

4. Place each cookie on a parchment-lined cookie sheet, ½ inch (1.25 cm) apart. Bake at 350°F (175°C) for 12 minutes or until the cookies are lightly golden around the edges.

5. Once they cool, it's time for the real fun: decorating (see page 60)!

*Recipe by Heather Coppersmith

RUSSIAN TEA CAKE* (makes 50 cookies)

This traditional holiday cookie is known by a number of different names—including Mexican Wedding Cake, Swedish Tea Cake, Italian Butter Nut, Southern Pecan Butterball, Snowdrop, and Viennese Sugar Ball. Whatever you choose to call these scrumptious little morsels, they will certainly be appreciated, so make a big batch.

5 ounces (142 g) toasted pecan pieces
1 cup (2 sticks, 226 g) butter
⅓ cup (65 g) granulated sugar
½ teaspoon (2.5 ml) vanilla
2 cups (240 g) all-purpose flour
½ teaspoon (2.5 ml) salt
Powdered sugar for rolling

1. Grind the toasted pecans to a fine powder.

2. Cream the butter and sugar until fluffy, then add the vanilla, flour, salt, and ground nuts.

3. Mix the ingredients until they're well incorporated and have formed a dough.

4. Scoop the dough into ¾-inch (2 cm) balls onto cookie sheets lined with parchment paper. Place 1 inch (2.5 cm) apart. Bake at 350°F (177°C) until light brown.

5. When cookies are cool, roll in a bowl of powdered sugar.

*Recipe by Heather Coppersmith

If you're giving cookies, be sure to present them nicely:
• individual brown paper bags tied with colorful curling ribbons

• a vintage tin (be sure to layer cookies between wax paper sheets)

• a pretty paper-wrapped box (don't forget the wax paper)

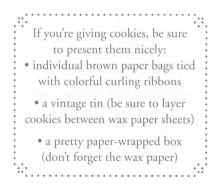

Throw a Cookie-Decorating Party

Set up a cookie-decorating station at your holiday party—kids will love it (and it will keep them happily occupied). Don't be surprised if grown-ups want to get in on the fun, too!

Kids will want to gobble up the cookies they've decorated, but if you can persuade them to set some aside, they'll make charming gifts for teachers. Don't forget to leave a few on a plate with a glass of milk for Santa.

COOKIE-DECORATING PARTY

Enough pre-baked sugar cookies in Christmas shapes (see recipe on page 58) for all of your guests to decorate at least one

Plate for each child

Paper or cloth towels

Royal icing (see recipe, opposite)

Small cups or bowls to hold decorative toppings

Decorative toppings: sprinkles, colored granulated sugar, mini-marshmallows, gumdrops

Freezer bags

Brown paper lunch bags

Ribbon

1. Set aside an entire afternoon for the event. You'll need to clear out a large surface area, like a counter or kitchen table, to act as the cookie-decorating station, plus a smaller spot where cookies can dry and set. Lay out all the necessary ingredients before the cookie party begins. You can set up the workstation assembly-line style, whereby each child can finish one job (frosting, adding sprinkles, dipping in chocolate), then pass it on to the next kid. Or you can set out all the ingredients in individual bowls and let the kids have at it, decorating their own cookies from start to finish.

2. Invite everyone to wash their hands first (or set out some hand-sanitizer towelettes).

3. The more variety of cookie shapes you have to decorate, the more opportunities for children to get creative.

4. After the decorating is complete, set the cookies aside on a baker's rack or parchment paper to allow the icing to harden for at least 1 hour. Then turn on a Christmas CD and let the kids burn off the sugar by dancing!

5. Finally, wrap up each child's cookies in brown paper lunch bags and tie with decorative ribbon (see page 79 for tips).

ROYAL ICING COOKIE-DECORATING BAGS

Royal icing gives cookies a smooth, satiny finish and will provide a pop of color if you add food coloring.

1. Beat 2 large egg whites and 2⅔ cups (270 g) powdered sugar with a wire whisk.

2. Working quickly before the icing dries, pour it into 4 or 5 different bowls, add different food colorings to each bowl, and mix again. If the icing seems too thin, add more powdered sugar.

3. Scoop each color of icing into individual freezer-weight plastic bags, twist until the icing is squeezed to one corner, then snip off the corner with a pair of scissors.

4. Show the kids how to use these homemade pastry bags to create designs on the cookies. Kids can use the frosting to draw an outline around the cookie, add polka dots, facial features, clothes, or designs. Fancy them up with sprinkles, sparkly sugar, and other decorative toppings.

Make Christmas Candy

An alternative to cookies, holiday candy makes a terrific hostess gift, workplace temptation, or homemade treat from your kitchen.

The varieties are endless, from super-easy to challenging: fudge, peanut brittle, peppermint bark, toffee, truffles, candied fruits, chocolate-covered pretzels, or whatever your sweet tooth desires. Decorative candy cups in metallic or holiday-printed paper add a refined touch.

TRUFFLES* *(makes approximately 50)*

The ultimate indulgence: bite-sized chocolate treats that absolutely melt in your mouth.

2 cups (475 ml) heavy whipping cream
12 ounces (340 g) dark chocolate (at least 60 percent cacao)
Cocoa powder for rolling
(optional) 1 tablespoon (15 ml) flavoring of your choice (rum, coffee liqueur, mint extract, orange extract).

1. Chop the chocolate into small pea-sized bits and place in a medium-sized bowl.

2. Heat the cream in a small saucepan until it barely begins to bubble.

3. Pour the hot cream over chocolate. With a whisk, stir the chocolate and cream together until it's all melted and smooth.

4. Add desired flavorings, but not more than 1 tablespoon total.

5. Cover the bowl in plastic and let it set overnight (or at least 4 hours).

6. With a truffle scoop or round spoon, scoop out the hardened filling onto a baking pan lined with parchment.

7. Roll each one in unsweetened cocoa powder, and pop them in your mouth, or place them on a serving dish or in a gift tin layered with wax paper.

*Recipe by Heather Coppersmith

CANDIED ORANGE PEELS

A work of art, candied orange peels are bright and beautiful, sweet and tart, and chewy yet crunchy. These sugary confections bring a bit of sunshine to your holiday.

4 navel or Valencia oranges
2¾ cups (550 g) granulated sugar

1. The best way to peel an orange for this purpose is to cut off the top and bottom, then score the skin into quarters, being careful not to cut into the pulp. Next, carefully peel the skin back. Once this is done, cut the peels into approximately ¼-inch (5 mm) slices.

2. Cover the orange peels in a large pan of water and bring to a boil. After letting it simmer on low heat for about 30 minutes, place the orange peels on a cookie sheet. You can repeat this step up to 4 times, depending on how strong you like the taste of the orange peel: the more often you boil them, the less tangy the taste becomes.

3. In another bowl, mix the sugar with 2 cups (475 ml) water, then let simmer on the stove for about 6 or 7 minutes.

4. Add the peels to the pan of simmering sugar water, and let them cook for about 45 minutes.

5. Drain the peels, then sugar the peels—either by rolling each peel in a pile of sugar or by placing them into a bag full of sugar and shaking well to make sure all the peels are coated.

6. Set on a platter to dry and cool for several hours or even a full day. Serve or store in an airtight container.

For the ultimate indulgence, dip the candied peels in melted milk chocolate or dark chocolate

Prepare Quick Family Dinners

Whip up these easy, foolproof recipes to keep your family nourished without spending all your time making meals.

ith so much going on during the holidays, it can be a challenge to put together a healthy, homemade dinner for your own family. Here are two recipes for hearty meals that will satisfy everyone and may even yield enough leftovers for another meal.

RATATOUILLE

This classic French comfort food is vegetarian, delicious, and easy to prepare.

Olive oil
1 large onion, quartered
1 eggplant cubed
2 red peppers, sliced
3 zucchini, unpeeled and chopped
4 tomatoes, chopped
Dash of salt, pepper, oregano, and thyme to taste

1. In a large saucepan, heat 2 teaspoons (10 ml) of olive oil. Sauté chopped onions until soft.

2. Add eggplant and red peppers and cook for about 10 minutes.

3. Add zucchini and tomatoes and cook for another 15 minutes.

4. Continue stirring and adding olive oil to prevent the vegetables from sticking to the bottom of the pan until all ingredients are cooked.

5. Serve alone or over bread or rice, melt Parmesan cheese on top, or use as a filling in an omelet.

> Ratatouille can be made a day in advance and is also great as leftovers

ONE-POT CHICKEN AND VEGETABLES*

A few minutes of preparation in the morning will guarantee a tasty, hearty meal by the time you arrive home at the end of the day. A slow cooker makes it easy.

4 medium potatoes
4 carrots
1 whole chicken
1 onion
6 cloves garlic
¼ cup (60 ml) lemon juice
¼ cup (60 ml) chicken stock
Salt and pepper to taste
Herbes de Provence (see recipe, below) to taste

1. Quarter the potatoes and peel and slice the carrots into 2-inch (5 cm) pieces, and place them at the bottom of the slow cooker.

2. Place the whole chicken on top of the vegetables with 2 quartered onions and 3 garlic cloves inside the chicken.

3. Pour the broth and lemon juice over the chicken. Add salt and pepper and herbes de Provence, and remaining onions and garlic.

4. Set the slow cooker for 8 hours on the low setting or cook for 2 hours in a Dutch oven at 325°F (165°C).

5. Serve by itself or with egg noodles or rice.

*Recipe by Lloyd Farnham

HERBES DE PROVENCE

You can buy prepared herbes de Provence—but it's easy to make your own version of this flavorful blend. Simply combine the following dried herbs:

1 teaspoon (5 ml) thyme   1 teaspoon (5 ml) marjoram
1 teaspoon (5 ml) ground rosemary   1 teaspoon (5 ml) basil
1 teaspoon (5 ml) summer savory   ½ teaspoon (2 ml) sage
½ teaspoon (2 ml) lavender   ½ teaspoon (2 ml) oregano

Combine all ingredients in an airtight container. (Makes a great gift, too!)

Lift Holiday Spirits

Lift holiday spirits with festive libations.

Stir up the holiday spirit by mixing up these classic libations sure to please your guests—or invent a signature holiday drink of your own and expect to be asked for the recipe.

HOMEMADE EGGNOG

The most iconic of holiday drinks, with a history that goes back to medieval England. Skip the store-bought carton and try mixing up this delicious, frothy, homemade version.

6 eggs, separated
½ cup (100 g) sugar
Nutmeg to taste
¼ teaspoon (1.25 ml) sea salt
2 tablespoons (30 ml) Tahitian vanilla
1 cup (240 ml) whole milk
2 cups (475 ml) heavy whipping cream
(optional) 1½ cups (350 ml) brandy or rum

1. In a bowl, beat egg yolks, along with ¼ cup (50 g) sugar, nutmeg, salt, and vanilla until the mixture has thickened.

2. Add the milk and continue beating.

3. Slowly beat in the rest of the sugar and the heavy whipping cream.

4. Add the egg whites and beat until you see frothy peaks.

5. Pour in the brandy (or rum) and gently mix the concoction together.

6. Ladle into mugs.

MULLED WINE

Heated and spiced, wine becomes a winter warmer and Christmas party favorite. Mulled wines have been enjoyed for centuries around the world. Versions are still popular today: in Sweden, they drink Glögg; in Germany, Glühwein; in France, vin brûlé. Mix up this recipe and serve in holiday mugs.

1 bottle red wine (some recipes suggest a fruity, medium-bodied red, but there are no rules and no need to spend a lot on the bottle)

1 peeled and sliced orange

6 cloves

¾ cup (175 ml) honey or ¾ cup (150 g) granulated sugar

4 cinnamon sticks

2 teaspoons (12 ml) vanilla

1. Combine all the ingredients into a large pot.

2. Warm on the stove over medium heat for less than 30 minutes, stirring frequently.

3. Once you see steam coming off the pan, you can start ladling it into cups to be enjoyed.

HOT SPICED CIDER

Popular since ancient times, apple cider is another beverage that heat and spices can transform into a holiday treat. No alcohol means this festive drink can be for all-ages.

2 teaspoons (10 ml) nutmeg

4 cinnamon sticks

1 teaspoon (5 ml) salt

1 teaspoon (5 ml) allspice

¼ cup (45 g) brown sugar

2 quarts (2 liters) apple cider

Mix all the ingredients in a large pot and warm it on the stove over medium heat for less than 30 minutes. Stir frequently, and serve when warm.

CHRISTMAS PUNCH

A special punch is more than a tasty excuse to pull that crystal punch bowl out of storage—it's a party in itself!

3 cups (700 ml) vodka

6 cups (1.5 liters) cranberry juice

2 cups (475 ml) lime juice

3 cups (700 ml) water

¼ cup (50 g) sugar

Pour the ingredients into a punch bowl, stir well, add ice cubes, and ladle into cups.

Serve Hors d'Oeuvres

Irresistible and inventive small bites give guests a scrumptious start to your holiday fête.

ors d'oeuvres—small bites meant to whet the appetite while staving off hunger—are a Christmas party staple. These delicious morsels may serve as the main act of your cocktail party or as exquisite pre-dinner temptations. Here are four simple yet sure-to-please canapés you can count on.

MARINATED GOAT CHEESE SPREAD*

½ jar sun-dried tomatoes, packed in oil and drained

1 log plain goat cheese

2 bunches of basil

2 cups (270 g) toasted pine nuts

1 garlic clove, cut into slivers

1. Soften the sun-dried tomatoes by steaming them for about 10 minutes, and slice them into long strips.

2. Cut the cheese log into 1-inch (2.5 cm) rounds.

3. In a tall Mason jar, start layering in the following order: cheese round, basil leaves, pine nuts, garlic, and sun-dried tomatoes, until all the ingredients have been incorporated.

4. Add olive oil to the Mason jar until it's full to the rim.

5. Serve spread on crackers.

*Recipe by David Noller

MINI-PANINI SANDWICHES*

1 loaf walnut or olive bread, thinly sliced

2 packages sliced prosciutto

Arugula

Fontina cheese

Olive Oil

1. On a slice of bread, layer the prosciutto, arugula, and cheese, then top with another slice of bread.

2. On a stovetop griddle or in a frying pan, drizzle olive oil and cook the sandwiches on medium heat, pressing down with a spatula.

3. Remove from heat, and slice the sandwich into either triangles or bite-size strips.

*Recipe by Heather Coppersmith

GRILLED POTATO SKEWERS*

Bamboo skewers

1 to 2 large bags baby new potatoes

Olive oil to taste

Freshly ground black pepper to taste

Ground thyme to taste

Oregano to taste

1 clove garlic, minced

1. Boil the potatoes for 20 minutes. This will soften them for grilling.

2. Cool potatoes under cold running water, then slice each potato in half.

3. Soak a set of bamboo skewers in water for 20 minutes. While the skewers are soaking, mix the olive oil, black pepper, thyme, oregano, and minced garlic.

4. Load potatoes onto a skewer, then brush with the flavored oil.

5. Cook the skewers on a stovetop griddle, and compress with a spatula to create those telltale horizontal lines on the potatoes. If you choose to, you can turn them 90 degrees and press them down again to make hash marks.

*Recipe by Christopher Coppersmith

FETA CHEESE SENSATION

8 ounces (225 g) Greek feta cheese

Fresh mint, tarragon, green onions, parsley all equaling ½ pound (225 g)

½ cup (125 ml) olive oil

8 ounces (225 g) ground walnuts

Pita bread

1. Grate the feta cheese (or cut into small squares), place it in a bowl, and cover with the olive oil.

2. Finely chop the herbs.

3. Add the herb mix and the ground walnuts to the bowl of feta, and blend together thoroughly.

4. Cut pitas into triangles, toast them until they're crispy, and place around a platter. Put the spread in a lovely bowl and place it in the center of the platter for dipping.

Plan Your Christmas Day Menu

It all leads up to this festive meal!

The centerpiece of the holiday is your main Christmas Day meal. For most, that meal is dinner, but you could also make it brunch or lunch—it's up to you to create the ideal tradition for your family. Whether everyone looks forward to the favorite family recipes or you like to experiment with different traditions or new directions, browse these menus for ideas on savory delights and sweet treats.

TRADITIONAL CHRISTMAS DINNER I

Succulent Roast Turkey

The ultimate Christmas staple roasted in the oven with stuffing and garnishes, and enjoyed with gravy. Try brining first to ensure a moist bird. Adding bacon and herbs during the long roast will result in a delicious taste.

Mashed Potatoes

The classic side dish, so satisfying and filling, so humble, and yet so easily transformed into a show-stopping winner. Add chives, horseradish, garlic, buttermilk, sour cream, paprika, rosemary, cheddar, or chicken broth, or go with just butter and a little gravy on top.

Brussels Sprouts

Roast with olive oil, sea salt, pepper, and grated parmesan. Or pour on a butter-and-brown-sugar sauce, topped off with walnuts. Or bake with chestnuts and cover with bread crumbs and butter.

Pecan Pie

The aroma of roasted pecans will vie for everyone's attention amongst all the other amazing scents of the day. The filling adds just the perfect shot of sweetness to this nutty treat.

TRADITIONAL CHRISTMAS DINNER II

Glazed Ham

A sweet glaze of mustard, brown sugar or maple syrup, and cloves makes a mouth-watering main dish that is a nice alternative to turkey.

Sweet Potatoes

Prepare au gratin, meld with polenta, purée with pear, whip into a soufflé, or caramelize in a maple glaze—sweet potatoes are always a crowd-pleaser.

Green Beans with Almonds

Another classic combination beloved by many. Consider adding mushrooms or pearl onions, or opt for an Asian touch with soy sauce.

Christmas Bread Pudding

Rich, custardy, and decadent. What began as "poor man's puddin'" hundreds of years ago has evolved into a favorite dessert, especially during the holidays. Try adding tart fruits like cranberries, chunks of chocolate, or citrus zest.

NEW TRADITIONS CHRISTMAS DINNER

A more adventurous selection, exciting for the foodies at your table while still pleasing to the traditionalists.

Leg of Lamb

Bake lamb with fragrant figs and lemon slices, or marinate it with rosemary, olive oil, garlic, and white wine and top it off with fresh herbs, like thyme or mint.

Beets

Bright red and beautiful! Drizzle with orange juice and serve alongside wedged lettuce as a salad; top with feta cheese and caramelized onions that have been whipped into a frothy soup; stuff with cabbage and nuts; or dice alongside cucumbers and tomatoes.

Maple-Glazed Turnips and Parsnips

Root vegetables, seasonal and substantial, are transformed by a sweet maple glaze.

Pumpkin Cheesecake

The gourmand take on the traditional pumpkin pie, this is a combination of two phenomenal desserts. Smooth as silk, light as a cloud, and packed with flavor. Use canned pumpkin purée or make your own. Either way, it will be a winner.

MOUTHWATERING VEGETARIAN MENU

For the non-carnivores in the group, choose a combination
of these satisfying and delectable dishes.

Vegetable Lasagna

This hearty meal can be customized a million different ways. In addition to
the prerequisite ricotta cheese, pile on the vegetables: mushrooms, spinach,
tomatoes, zucchini, squash, onions, and broccoli.

Vegetable Shepherd's Pie

Revisit this hearty staple as a meat-free dish by using lots of vegetables
(any combination of carrots, onions, eggplants, peppers, or other faves), plus
some hearty grains (barley is a great choice) and legumes (lentils work nicely).
Top the whole thing with a layer of creamy mashed potatoes, and even the
meat-eaters at your table will be clamoring for a portion.

Mushroom Stroganoff

Use a mix of substantial, flavorful mushrooms, including portobello, porcini,
oyster, and button for a rich and creamy combination served atop a mound of
satisfying egg noodles.

Winter Greens

The bounty of the holiday season comes in the form of winter greens, and
when combined with the right spices and herbs, they can win over even the
most stubborn vegetable foe. Collect them in heaps and pounds: spinach,
kale, mustard greens, Swiss chard, arugula, and collards. Braise them or
sauté them with garlic and olive oil or a splash of red wine vinegar or balsamic
vinegar, and mix in some bacon for that extra dose of flavor.

Squash

Whether it's butternut, spaghetti, kabocha, delicata, or acorn, each type
has its own distinct consistency and taste. Scoop out the innards and
slice and grill; sauté with herbs and spices; or stuff and bake with other
goodies, like nuts and onions.

Apple Brown Betty

Cinnamon and nutmeg add excitement, and baking this dish will send an
irresistible aroma through the house. Add a rich vanilla ice cream.

CHRISTMAS BRUNCH

Why wait until the late afternoon or evening to feast? Brunch can be an equally festive event, and it leaves the afternoon free for socializing, visiting, sports, or your family's idea of a good time.

Bacon and Cheese Frittata

Much easier to make than a quiche and great for feeding a group of people, use fontina or goat cheese in this recipe, and you'll have a smash hit with your guests. Add mushrooms if you're feeling guilty about the lack of vegetables.

Eggs Benedict

The classic crowd-pleaser: poached eggs sitting on warm biscuits, toast, or English muffins, with a few delicately thin slices of ham in between. Don't forget to top off with a delicious hollandaise sauce.

Bacon or Sausage

Every brunch must have one or the other, if not both! Not only will you get the unbeatable taste, there's also the tantalizing aroma.

Cranberry Coffee Cake

Adding a dash of sweet flavor to complement the savory dishes, this can be served warm or at room temperature.

Fruit Salad

Throw in your favorites: sliced apples, bananas, melons, strawberries, or whatever fresh fruits you can find at the grocery store, then squeeze the juice of an orange over the entire blend to sweeten it. Also offer plain yogurt, granola, and muesli to your guests to mix with the fruit.

For inspiration, consult your favorite cookbooks. Start early in the season, so you'll have plenty of time to experiment with your menu. Visit websites of your favorite cooking magazines and television shows for more ideas; the Web is a fantastic resource for recipes, reviews, and feedback.

chapter

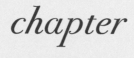

GIVING

Add meaning to the holidays by making your gifts.

C ounting down the days until Christmas is an exciting time. But the weeks leading up to the holiday can be spoiled by worries about finding (and paying for) the perfect gift for everyone on your list. This pressure makes the countdown more of a stressful reminder of all that remains to be done. As retail shops unleash their most aggressive sales tactics, you may feel you must take advantage of "sales." The compulsion to buy sends you to the mall to pile on the ties, sweaters, gloves, and soaps, hoping to match the right item to someone on your list, while accruing debt. Despite all your good intentions, you end up feeding the buy-and-give cycle that invariably results in unwanted items being tossed into an ever-growing dump.

＊

Take a moment to stop and consider how to put an end to this rut. What does gift giving mean to you? For most of us, it's a way to connect with friends and family, to show them that you care about them, to let them know you're thinking about what they like, and to share a piece of yourself. Buying anonymous, undistinguished presents is actually the antithesis of what you're trying to achieve by gift giving. Consider how appreciative you are when someone presents you with a handmade gift. Instead of gift giving becoming a dreaded and expensive chore, it can become a chance to reconnect with those you care about.

＊

This year, try making your holiday presents. This chapter offers ideas for simple, homemade gifts that you can specifically tailor for your recipients. You don't have to be an expert crafter or have lots of spare time to make these gifts—you need only the willingness to sit down and focus for an hour or two here and there—and before you know it, you'll have homemade gifts for everyone on your list—and you'll have enjoyed the process, too.

✳

In this chapter, you'll find a list of projects anyone can do, such as a homemade photo album (great for extended family members), a mixed CD (you must know some music lovers), framed art by your own little artist (ideal for relatives), and some easy bookmarks (for the readers on your list). If you're willing to be a little more crafty, you'll have no trouble with simple stamped stationery, easy earrings, or a throw pillow. You'll also find instructions for gifts you can knit, sew, or felt. If you're more comfortable in the kitchen, we offer ideas for olive oil infusions or a collection of your own best recipes; if the garden is where you feel at home, read the suggestions for plants and planters to give. For any gift, try the eco-friendly, creative wraps included in this chapter.

✳

Finally, and in the spirit of Christmas, consider giving the ultimate gift: your time. From charitable offerings to helping out those in need to sharing your knowledge, a gift of your time may be the most meaningful of all.

Infuse Olive Oil

Personalize a kitchen condiment with herbs.

Gifts from and for the kitchen are useful and always appreciated. And it's not necessary to be an expert chef to make these gifts. The olive oil infusion is an easy and thoughtful gift that will be regularly used in the kitchen. All the cooks amongst your friends and family will love you for it, because it's something everyone wants to do, but rarely has the time for.

1. Decide what flavors you want to infuse into your oil. Good options include tarragon, basil, thyme, rosemary, cilantro, oregano, chive, mint, dill, or parsley.

2. Wash and dry the herbs. Use a mortar and pestle to grind them loosely.

3. Choose a decorative glass or ceramic bottle. Drop your ground herbs (and add a couple whole sprigs so the herb is identifiable) into the bottle and, using a funnel, pour in the oil. Seal the bottle tightly.

✳ Infused oils must be refrigerated.

✳ The new concoction can be used to dress salads; marinate meats, fish, and vegetables; and as a dip for a nice loaf of bread.

You can add a homemade flavor to many kitchen staples using herbs.

• **Fill tea sachets:** With your favorite blends—chamomile, peppermint, anise, or other herbal leaves—put together a package of 6 or 8 sachets.

• **Concoct your own herbed salt and poultry rubs:** Add herbs like rosemary, tarragon, oregano, basil, garlic, chives, thyme, dill, or paprika.

• **Raise a glass with a homemade vodka infusion:** A single flavor will work or try a blend like cucumber, cantaloupe, and apples.

Present Gifts from the Kitchen

A gift made with love deserves an equally heartfelt presentation.

Your cookies are decorated, your truffles have set, and your olive oil is infused. Now it's time to package up the food gifts from your kitchen (and your heart) with style. Earth-friendly and stylish options abound.

LINERS

Be sure to use food-safe liners or packaging to hold gifts from your kitchen. Then place your safely wrapped gifts into other containers.

Parchment and wax papers: These papers are completely food-safe, reusable, compostable, and non-toxic when incinerated—look for unbleached brands. Also, avoid parchment made with the chemical, Quilon; silicone is safe and biodegradable.

Aluminum foil: 100 percent recycled foil can be purchased, and it is recyclable in most regions. Do note that it may react with salty and acidic foods.

PACKAGING

Tins: Old-fashioned yet functional, tins are great for gifting cookies and sweets. Simply tie one up with a bow or wrap it in recycled paper or a square of scrap fabric.

Glass jars and bottles: Perfect for homemade preserves, jams, and infusions, jars and bottles can easily be collected throughout the year. Cover the lid with a piece of fabric, secure it with a rubber band, and disguise the rubber band with a cute ribbon.

Bags: Any decoration will enhance and complement a recyclable brown paper bag. After you've folded closed the top of the bag, punch holes and weave ribbon through them. Or place your gift in a cloth bag that can be redeployed as an everyday shopping bag.

Fabric: Think fabric remnants, dish towels, aprons, and even oven mitts. See page 103 for tips on wrapping with fabric (furoshiki).

Compile a Cookbook

You may not be able to cook for your friends as often as you'd like, but you can give them your recipes!

Finding that perfect dinner recipe—easy, fast, and delicious—is like discovering the Holy Grail for busy people. If you've hit upon a trove of jackpot recipes—for dinner or another meal—sharing them with your friends is the ultimate gift.

As with any gift, think of the recipients and what type of recipes they would appreciate most. Consider whether they're vegetarian, vegan, lactose intolerant, or have other dietary restrictions. Then share the wealth!

Family heirlooms: For your siblings and cousins, you can put together a book of old family recipes that have been passed around among cousins, aunts, uncles, parents, and grandparents.

Delicious desserts: Dessert is always in demand! If you've found the perfect recipe for chocolate chip cookies or the most winning tiramisu, you can design a dessert theme for your recipe book.

Dinner party planners: For those blessed with friends who love to entertain, put together a recipe book that lists a menu of hors d'oeuvres, entrees, and desserts, complete with wine pairings. And if you really want to share all your secrets to the successful dinner party, include a list of your greatest musical hits, too.

Interactive cooking: Save paper and go digital—sign onto a recipe-sharing website, upload your favorite recipes and send the links to your friends. Once they're signed up, they can peruse your recipes, and add their own—a bonus for you!

Whether you handwrite each recipe or type and print them out, you'll want to present them in an appealing way.

- Write your recipes in a pretty blank book or journal.
- Present the recipes on a set of hand-decorated cards tied with a colored ribbon or piece of twine.
- Embellish a tin or box and place your recipes on cards inside.
- Take photos of finished dishes and include them with the recipes.
- Ask your kids to draw pictures of their favorite recipes to decorate each page or card.

Put Together a Picture Book

A photo album is a thoughtful gift for family and friends who live far away.

The photo album or scrapbook is a beloved holiday tradition for good reason—it captures moments and allows them to be relived and enjoyed over and over again, especially for loved ones you don't see as often as you'd like. You can choose from a variety of albums, papers, and decorative additions to create an album that reflects your style and personality.

For a special family member or friend, an album is a welcome gift. You can make it as simple or lavish as you'd like. An eight-page collection of great images will be appreciated, so don't feel you must wait until you have tons of images.

Themed album: Choose images of an event of importance in your life this year—a new baby, a vacation or trip, a graduation, an anniversary or birthday, or any special occasion you'd like to remember. Inscribe it with a personal message.

Yearbook: Relive the year past with photos of the main events. A brief description of who's in each image, where and when it was taken, and any memories you'd like to share will make it special.

Life in pictures: Put the spotlight on someone special—your grandfather, a favorite aunt, a cherished family friend, or even a pet—to be the star of the album. It could be a retrospective of someone's entire life, complete with memories. Alternatively, you could focus on a special accomplishment or experience and create a short memory book.

Family calendar: Turn your images into a calendar with a new photo for every month. Software, websites, and templates are available to help you with this project—or do it completely by hand.

If you are more digital than analog, there are numerous photo album sites that allow you to create albums and print them as books or send links to those with whom you'd like to share. A digital album means you can share with everyone on your list at once.

kid friendly

Mix a CD

Making a favorite music mix is as much a labor of love for you as it is a treasured gift.

gift of music is a gift of joy. Sharing music that is meaningful to you is a personal and easy way to spread the joy to your loved ones, showing that you took the time and effort to create something unique.

To make a successful mix, first decide upon the overall approach: Are you an aficionado who wants to share your latest finds? Do you want to give a particular friend a playlist that reflects something you have shared or that you think will resonate with her? Or maybe you have a fun theme in mind and want to share it with all your friends? Once you've made this choice, the rest of the project will come together quickly.

Playlist: Consider your recipients. Are you making a single mix for everyone this year or do you want to create unique musical experiences for each person on your list? As long as you're sitting at the computer and have your playlist open, you can easily make half a dozen CDs in an afternoon. Consider: Your best friend (swoons for the jazz greats), your sibling (loves indie bands), your mother (looks for any excuse to dance), your neighbor (needs the perfect blood-thumping mix for her marathon training), and even your kid's teacher (prefers a relaxing suite of piano sonatas).

Details: Be sure to make a list of each song and artist for the listener to follow. Handwrite and decorate or type and print it out, then tuck into the sleeve with the CD.

Presentation: Make your own sleeve or purchase a pack of them; you can then embellish to make it as fancy or simple as you like.

Important last note: Come up with a great album title appropriate to the mix.

> If you absolutely don't have time to burn CDs, you can put together a playlist and print it out on nice paper or handwrite it on a card, and offer it with a gift certificate to an online music site like iTunes or Amazon.

kid friendly

Stamp Stationery

Encourage the lost art of writing with pen and paper by making personalized, ready-to-use stationery.

Emails, texts, tweets, and blogs may have taken over most of our communications, but people still like to write and receive tangible correspondence. Of course, a person might be more inclined to write letters if some homemade stationery is on hand.

Personalized notes: Start with a set of six blank note cards or sheets of good quality paper. Make or purchase some simple stamps with your recipient's initials (see page 15 for how to make your own stamps). Practice your design on a scrap, then stamp your design across the top of the paper or in the center of the front of the card. You can add an additional stamp design—it could be a holiday motif or another image the recipient will appreciate. Include a set of stamps to really spark some creativity!

Custom journal: Everyone needs some kind of notebook, from the daily journal writer to the to-do list jotter, and blank notebooks are just begging to be customized. Choose a notebook that suits your recipient's style. If the cover is made of paper, you can stamp his initials or your design directly onto the cover. If it's made of leather or another type of material, you can make labels and affix them to the book.

Try other decorative techniques to create your custom stationery, like embossing, stickers, applique, painting, or decoupage.

Make Bookmarks

A book is always a thoughtful and rewarding gift.

o make the gift more personal, insert a fabulous homemade bookmark into each book you give. You can easily make a dozen or more of these little placeholders in a sitting, if you think creatively.

All you need is pretty paper, plain card stock, glue, and a 3-inch (7.5 cm) piece of ribbon. This is a terrific way to use up those scraps of cool paper you've been saving. Almost any kind of paper will work—textured Japanese paper, wallpaper scraps, wrapping paper, or old postcards.

1. Cut your card stock and paper into 2- by 6-inch (5 x 15 cm) rectangles.

2. Glue the paper onto the card stock.

3. Punch a hole at the top and tie a ribbon through it for an extra bit of embellishment.

4. Trim the edges neatly.

5. If you want your bookmarks to last, get them laminated.

6. Tuck a bookmark in the pages of a book before you wrap it, or affix it to the outside of the wrap or bow for a decorative touch.

> For the true book-lovers on your list, you might want to make a special addition to the bookmark in the form of a favorite book list. Jot down your favorite books from the past year or two, note the authors, and give a little synopsis of each one or a brief sentence about why you loved it. Include with holiday cards or slip into other presents—or just hand them out to friends and family!

Say It in Thread

Use needle and thread to express yourself.

G iving a piece of original handiwork as a gift is the ultimate compliment. It means you think well enough of the recipient to spend your valuable time creating something she'll appreciate. When it comes to stitching, embroidery is a simple and elegant craft that instantly turns even the simplest designs into art.

Puppies and mountain scenes are not the only designs you'll find for embroidery patterns. You can choose from readymade designs widely available, or you can easily sketch a line drawing of an image of your choice: a silhouette of a girl, the Eiffel Tower, a snowman, or letters of the alphabet. Try your handiwork on a T-shirt, baby onesie, handkerchief, pillowcase, handbag, scarf, or any other fabric. It will be as unique and original as anything that hangs on a wall.

1. Use tracing paper and a water-soluble pen or pencil to transfer your design to your fabric. (The markings will wash out.)

2. Use a simple running or stem stitch to outline your design in embroidery floss or wool.

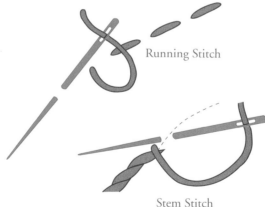

Running Stitch

Stem Stitch

Create a Pair of Earrings

Bedeck your friends' earlobes with simple yet lovely baubles.

ith a selection of carefully curated beads, stones, or metal or wooden charms, you can create beautiful stud earrings in a matter of minutes.

A bead shop or craft store is likely to be your one-stop shop for everything you need, including high-quality, non-irritating posts with backs (stainless steel, gold, or silver are safe options), every bead and bauble you can imagine, and the proper glue you'll need to adhere the bauble to the post (you might need different glues depending on the composition of your chosen materials).

1. If the bauble has a slick surface, roughen the back with a file so the glue will have a stronger hold.

2. Clean the surface with rubbing alcohol before applying the glue.

3. Apply the glue either to the post or to the bauble. Since you are working with a small surface area, use a toothpick to avoid any messiness.

4. Let the glue dry completely.

5. Wrap the earrings in tissue paper, then place in a cute box or a small fabric bag tied with a ribbon.

> It's easiest if you pick baubles with relatively flat backs for successful adherence to the earring posts. However, if you prefer a rounded bead, there are cupped earring posts available just for this purpose. Investigate all of your options and keep your friends' personal styles in mind when choosing materials.

Felt

Repurpose an old sweater into a cool new scarf or pot holder.

Felting gives wool a tighter, flatter texture that is very appealing. It requires only a washer and dryer and is amazingly easy. Though these projects will win you amazingly high marks for creativity and effort, they will take just a few minutes to finish.

FELTED SCARF*

1. Choose a 100 percent wool sweater you no longer wear.

2. Wash and dry the sweater on the hottest settings.

3. Using sharp scissors, trim off the hem along the bottom, and cut a continuous spiral around your sweater about 6 inches (15 cm) wide. The ideal scarf length for an adult is about 4 feet (1.2 m) long.

4. Now add on the embellishments—here is one to try: weave a contrasting-colored yarn through the scarf by cutting notches along the edges about 1 inch (2.5 cm) apart and threading the yarn through.

FELTED POT HOLDER*

1. Now that you've got the hang of felting, try a felted pot holder. Felt your sweater as in Steps 1 and 2 above.

2. Cut two 7-inch (18 cm) squares from the sweater (or two sweaters, for contrasting patterns) and round off the corners.

3. Stack the squares with the right sides facing out.

4. Using embroidery floss, sew a blanket stitch around the entire perimeter of the pot holder.

*Projects by Tiffany Threadgould

Sock a Monkey

If you have even a bit of inclination to sew, a sock monkey's an easy and extremely gratifying project with lots of opportunity to customize.

Sock monkeys have come a long way since their inception in 1932. Recently, these hand-sewn cuties have been popping up everywhere, from haute design shops to craft fairs. Something about those loosey-goosey limbs makes them instantly lovable. They seem to be saying, "Hug me!"

1. You'll need a pair of socks that are in good condition, preferably with a dense knit in either cotton or wool. One sock will make up the head, body, and legs, while the other sock will be the arms, tail, mouth, and ears of your monkey.

2. Turn both socks inside out.

3. To make the legs, body, and head, flatten the sock so the heel is in the center facing up. With a fabric pen, draw a line in the middle from 1 inch (2.5 cm) or so above the heel all the way through the top (cuff) for the legs. The heel of the sock will be the monkey's behind, and the foot will be the body and head.

4. With a sewing machine, sew a straight line down the right side ½ inch (1 cm) from your marked line, and then sew a straight line ½ inch (1 cm) down the left side of the center line. When you reach the cuff on both sides, make sure to round out your stitching to make little, closed feet.

5. Cut straight along your marked line between the two sewn lines. Now, you have two monkey legs.

6. Turn the sock right side out and fill (very well) with stuffing, using the hole that has been conveniently left open in the crotch. A pencil, chopstick, or knitting needle is helpful in evenly distributing the stuffing.

7. Sew up the hole in the crotch as cleanly as you can. Make sure there are no raw edges visible.

8. With the other sock, draw the ears, mouth, arms, and tail onto the sock (see illustration), and cut out the pieces.

9. Sew the arm and tail pieces closed, turn right side out, and stuff to desired thickness.

10. Securely attach the arms and tail to your monkey body.

11. Attach the mouth. It is going to seem big for your monkey's face, but that is fine because you will be stuffing it for definition. Do your best to create a nice oval shape.

12. Stuff the mouth and stitch it closed.

13. Stitch the ears closed and then attach them to the sides of the head.

14. Sew buttons on the face as the two eyes.

15. Now you've got a lovable, huggable monkey that will melt anyone's heart.

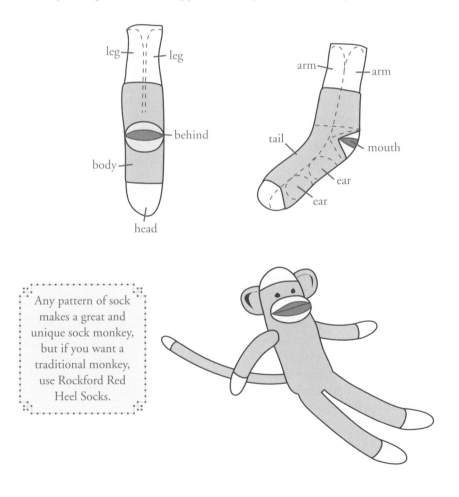

Any pattern of sock makes a great and unique sock monkey, but if you want a traditional monkey, use Rockford Red Heel Socks.

Sew a Throw Pillow

Use your sewing skills to add a pop of color and pattern with a homemade throw pillow.

Everyone loves a pretty throw pillow—it can go almost anywhere in the house: on the bed in the bedroom, on the sofa or reading chair in the living room, or on the floor in the kids' room. A trip to the fabric store or a look into your own stash of fabrics will give you all the inspiration you need for this simple project. If you don't want to start from scratch, you can re-cover an existing pillow; the instructions below will work for either project.

1. Decide what room and purpose you intend the pillow for, and choose your fabric(s) accordingly.

2. Measure the pillow insert and mark the fabric so that the pieces you cut will have a ¼-inch (5 mm) seam allowance. Cut two pieces of fabric the same size (they can be the same fabric or different).

3. Put the two pieces front to front. With the fabric wrong side up, sew along three sides. You can do this by hand or with a sewing machine.

4. If you're re-covering an existing pillow or using a pre-bought pillow insert, turn the fabric right side out, then fit your pillow into the opening of the pocket you've just sewn. Now sew the fourth side together from inside the pillow. To do this, fold the edges of the fabric down to make a smooth edge. Stitch along one side of the fabric, then sew it together with the other side of the fabric and pull the two sides tight. Repeat until you're at the end and tie off.

If you're using stuffing, sew halfway to the end with a sewing machine or by hand, then tie off, leaving a 6-inch (15 cm) opening on the fourth side. Turn the fabric right-side out and stuff your stuffing into the opening, making sure to reach all corners of the pillow; the more stuffing you can get in there, the fluffier the pillow will be. When it's stuffed to capacity, fold over the fabric and hand sew the opening together from the inside of the pillow, as described above.

Sow Seeds

With its unlimited potential, a gift of seeds may be the definitive gift that keeps on giving.

Among the most rewarding ways to reduce your carbon footprint is to grow your own plants, flowers, and vegetables. Whether they're practical or decorative, they bring life to your windowsill or yard and can even improve the air quality inside your home. You can easily make a seedling kit to suit anyone on your list.

1. At the garden shop, buy a packet of your favorite flower or herb seeds, a bag of rich, composted soil, and small biodegradable pots.

2. For a lovely presentation, fill a pot with soil, top it off with a bit of straw to keep the soil in place, and place the packet of seeds on top. Tie a pretty ribbon around the whole package.

✳ For an even greener and more homemade solution, make your own biodegradable pots. Cardboard egg cartons are ready to use as soon as you poke a hole in the bottom of each cup and they can be put right into the ground as is. Toilet paper rolls and newspaper can both be snipped and folded into seedling pots that can be planted (see Resources on page 124).

> If you're feeling motivated, try cultivating an indoor herb garden in advance, so the plants are ready for use in the kitchen when you give it to your recipient.

Make Mini Masterpieces (with the Kids)

kid friendly

It's never too early to teach a child the immense pleasure of making a homemade gift.

Children of all ages can make Christmas gifts. With a little help from mom, dad, or an older sibling, a child can make a present and feel proud about the accomplishment.

FOR THE VERY YOUNG

Every child is an emerging artist; whether your Picasso is going to turn out to be the next big thing in the art world is anyone's guess. Regardless, his or her early works are precious enough for relatives, so why not help your little one make a painting for someone who'd love to have it?

1. Set up a painting station with a set of watercolors or poster paints and any other art supplies your child likes and is familiar with, as well as some quality painting paper.

2. Let your child create his masterpiece. Try not to direct it too much, so that the piece is unique to the child's personality.

3. When it's dry, have your child autograph the bottom of the paper.

4. Ask your child to name or describe the work, and neatly pencil in the title next to her name.

5. The most important part: Invest in a good frame with matting and place the work of art inside.

6. Now beam with pride!

> You can buy small canvases from most art supply shops. Your child can paint directly onto the canvas. It looks very professional and it's ready to hang as soon as it's dry.

FOR THE BIGGER KID

If your child can use safety scissors and tacky glue comfortably, a whole new world of crafts is about to unfold. Try a simple decorated picture frame—it's a gift that almost everyone on your list can use.

1. For this project, you'll need a simple wooden frame, which you can find at most craft stores. In a pinch, make one with 4 large craft sticks (also readily available—they look like Popsicle sticks).

2. You'll need some decorative elements to glue around edges—raid your craft supplies or go on the hunt for a pile of any of the following: buttons, shells, macaroni (any fun pasta shapes will work; you could spray them silver first for a shiny look), or even small toys. Alternatively, you can cut out shapes from craft foam or construction paper.

3. Help your child dab a small blob of tacky glue on the back of the item to be attached; press firmly to the front of the frame.

4. Let dry completely. Leave the frame empty, or have your child pick a favorite photo to complement his work of art.

FOR THE BIG KID

Most of the projects in this book can be done by tweens and teens, with just a bit of guidance from an adult, from stitching to paper craft. You might also encourage an experiment with homemade gifts from the kitchen—kids generally like to eat sweets, so why not let them bake some simple treats to give? Discovering how rewarding it is to give a gift made with your own hands is a gift in itself, and one you can easily share with your child.

kid friendly

Transform a Planter with Mosaic

Create art with tiles, beads, shells, and faux jewels.

The ancient art of mosaic—applying pieces of ceramic, glass, or stone to a surface to create an image or pattern—can be applied to almost any item. Mosaic is a terrific activity for older kids. Try transforming a plain flower pot—it's the ideal utilitarian gift that can be used over and over again.

1. Find a terra cotta pot from your own collection, or pick one up from a home or hardware store.

2. Rifle through your arts and crafts supplies or jewelry box and look for pretty jewels, stones, marbles, shells, or beads. Colored tile and glass broken into pieces are also excellent options (just make sure to be very careful when handling jagged edges).

3. Once you've accumulated all of your pieces, spread a thick layer of grout over the entire pot.

4. While the grout is still fresh, press the pieces securely into the grout.

5. Add another thin layer of grout over the entire pot to fill the gaps.

6. When the grout has dried, take a wet sponge and wipe off all of the residual chalky grout for a smooth finish.

7. You're done! For an extra special touch, present the newly beautified pot pre-planted. You can find suggestions for holiday plants on page 36.

Give a Practical Basket

For the person who has everything, the gift of convenience might just be the perfect offering.

racticality goes a long way during the holidays, when preparations can be intensive and to-do lists overwhelming. A gift basket of necessities provides a welcome shot of humor and wish fulfillment.

The key to making this gift of practicality work is to target the right person and give things that are certain to be useful in that particular household.

Find a reusable storage box with a nice design. It could be a vintage crate, a woven basket, or a sturdy paper-covered box. Look in your own house and cupboards for inspiration—anything that regularly needs restocking, ingredients that you wish you had the last time you checked, necessities for a specific room, or even items for your car.

Household staples basket: Batteries, paper towels, light bulbs, dishwashing liquid, trash bags, vacuum bags, floor cleaner, sponges, dish towels.

Car necessities basket: Motor oil, windshield wiper fluid, air filter, a first-aid kit, flashlight, blanket, bottled water, emergency food.

No-time-to-make-dinner basket: Olive oil, tomato sauce, pasta, salad dressing.

Bath supplies basket: Toothpaste, soap, hand lotion, cotton balls, shampoo, conditioner.

Kids' art basket: Kid-safe scissors, glue, construction paper, washable markers, stickers.

Master the Art of Regifting

The number one rule for happy regifting: Keep track of who gave you what so that you never regift anything back to the original giver.

Here's the truth about regifting: If done right, there's absolutely no shame in it. In fact, it's completely preferable to buying an anonymous, mass-made product destined to become landfill—and it perfectly exemplifies the notion of reduce, reuse, and recycle. So go for it…but thoughtfully!

THE RULES OF REGIFTING:

∗ Be certain the object in question is totally appropriate for and would be welcomed by the recipient. Think about whether your intended would truly choose this item for him- or herself.

∗ Keep in mind your circle of friends, and whether the original giver and new receiver might ever meet or discover the regift. If it seems possible, reconsider. Make one of the easy and quick homemade projects in this book instead.

∗ You may regift only new, unopened items that are in pristine condition. If you opened it or used it, even just once, it should remain yours or be given to charity.

∗ Never regift a handmade item. It was made just for you, and you should keep it.

∗ Be sure the package is free of any original gift tags and prices, then rewrap it yourself.

If you follow these rules scrupulously, you should be able to find happy homes for those items that you've received but never used. If regifting them doesn't feel right, there are other options.

∗ Host a pre-holiday swap meet to which guests bring good-quality items they have no need for.

∗ Go online and Freecycle your items.

∗ Find a local charity that would benefit from your unused gifts.

Give to Charity

'Tis the season to give ... to those in need.

Amidst all the parties, gift giving, and celebrating, Christmas is also the ideal time to think about how to give to those who need help the most. Try to redirect all the effort put into mindless consumption and obligatory gifts into a task that will truly make an impact on someone's life. But where to start? Here are a few suggestions and guidelines.

Donate in someone's name as your gift to that person: Consider what organization the recipient might be interested in helping. Has he or she ever expressed interest in a specific cause?

Make a family gift: Ask your parents and siblings if they'd be interested in contributing as a family instead of, or in addition to, giving to each other.

Involve the kids: Give your children an opportunity to participate by offering them an amount of money to donate at Christmastime. Collect the various solicitations you receive by mail and online, review them with your children, and let them decide where they'd like to give.

Act locally: A lot of after-school programs collect letters from disadvantaged kids who ask for specific Christmas presents. Request a few of those letters and fulfill the children's wishes. Or contact your local utility company about paying a utility bill for a family who is having trouble keeping financially afloat.

Opt for an online gift: Most large and internationally well-known organizations make it easy to make a one-time or repeating gift online. Options include The Red Cross, Oxfam, Doctors Without Borders, Unicef, World Wildlife Fund, Greenpeace, Sierra Club, Earthjustice, Natural Resources Defense Council, or The Nature Conservancy.

Make sure the charity you're interested in is reputable. Several organizations monitor charities, including the Better Business Bureau Wise Giving Alliance, Charity Navigator, and the American Institute of Philanthropy.

Give a Gift of Time

Christmas is a great time to share your talent, skill, or knowledge that could benefit others.

As long as we are rethinking giving, consider how to share one of the most valuable things you have to give: your time. It's an easy-on-your-budget yet thoughtful alternative to more stuff—and you can scale it up or down depending on what you have to give and the recipients' needs. Decide what services you have to offer—to your family and friends and to the world at large—and pay it forward.

You'll want to present your gift in a formal way, so the recipient has something to open. Find a nice card and put the offer in writing, or make a cute, homemade gift certificate offering your unique services.

Babysitting or homework help: Offer busy parents a night away from the kids. Let them go for dinner and a movie! They will be forever grateful.

Pet walking or sitting: One of the hardest parts about going on vacation, especially for dog and cat owners, is figuring out what to do with a beloved pet. Offer to stay with an animal at your friend's home, to keep the animal at your own home, or to check in daily for feeding and walking.

Photography: If you're a natural shutterbug, offer to take portraits of your recipient and his or her family, siblings, partner, or pets. If someone you know has an event coming up—a birthday party, for example—you could offer to capture it in photos.

Organizing: Offer to de-clutter a home office, thin out an overstuffed closet, clean up a disastrous garage, or organize a disheveled pantry.

Packing and moving: Moving isn't fun for anyone, so helping out with this task will not only make it go faster but will also be more fun for everyone involved.

Painting or minor carpentry: Put on your overalls and help a not-so-handy friend add a coat of fresh paint to a dingy room or fix a much-needed repair around the house.

Refinishing furniture: If you're handy with stains and sandpaper, offer to return your aunt's favorite chair to its original glory.

Tech help: Upgrading your system, starting a blog, or creating a website might come second nature to you, but to someone else, it's the equivalent of speaking a foreign language. Help them out with your tech savvy.

Gardening: Plant a small vegetable, herb, or flower garden for a friend who's longing for some greenery but doesn't have the time or know-how to do it. Choose easy-care plants. This gift will keep on giving long after you've spent an afternoon setting it up.

Cooking: Don't just offer a gift certificate to a restaurant; instead, offer a delicious home-cooked meal, including appetizer, entrée, and dessert. You can make it a special date at your house or suggest cooking in the recipient's kitchen. Alternatively, offer to show a pal exactly how to make a favorite dish.

Resumé help: Help pull together a professional resumé. Depending on your own experience, you can help with everything from improving the overall look of the document to proofreading and editing content.

Driving: Save your buddy taxi fare with an offer to drive when it's needed: to the airport, on an errand, or to an appointment.

Lessons: Are you a piano player? A sailor? A knitter? A tennis pro? A ballroom dancer? These are hobbies that many of your friends and family would love to learn from you. Offer to host a weekend or evening "workshop" to show people how to get started.

Transferring music: There are many people for whom transferring music seems like something they'd need a new degree for. If you're up-to-speed, why not offer to help them move CDs (or cassette tapes or even, ahem, records) to a new system? Be sure to show them how it works and leave easy-to-follow instructions.

Artistry: If you are lucky enough to possess an artistic talent, offer your services for designing a logo or an invitation, painting a mural in a child's bedroom, or sewing a prom dress.

Knit a Hat

The ultimate expression of love is a knitted goodie.

Knitting a project usually requires a big time commitment. There are some projects, however, that a reasonably competent knitter can whip up in one sitting, like this hat, which can be adapted for either gender. If you're a fast knitter who likes to keep busy while watching television or riding the bus, you may be able to outfit several people on your list.

COZY WINTER HAT *

Directions are for a woman's hat. Changes for a man's hat are in parentheses. Finished hat circumference is 20 inches or 50 cm (23 inches or 57.5 cm).

Yarn: 2 (2) balls of 3 ounce (85 g) wool or acrylic yarn. If you wish to add a contrasting stripe, add 1 ball of a contrasting color.

Gauge: 21 sts & 30 rows = 4 inch (10 cm) in stockinette stitch.

Knitting Needles: size 6 (4 mm) for main hat, size 4 (3.5 mm) for ribbing.

To knit the hat:

With smaller needles, cast on 108 (120) sts.

✳ Row 1: *k2, p2; repeat from * across

✳ Row 2: *p2, k2: repeat from * across

✳ Repeat these 2 rows until piece measures 3 inches or 7.5 cm. Change to size 6 (4 mm) needles and stockinette stitch. Work even until piece measures 6½ inches or 16.25 cm (7 inches or 17.5 cm).

To shape the crown:

✳ Row 1: k 8 (9), *k2tog, k 16 (18), slip 1, k 1, pass slipped st over the knit st, k 16 (18); repeat from * across, ending with k 8 (9).

✳ Row 2: k 7 (8), *k2tog, k 15 (17), slip 1, k 1, pass slipped st over the knit st, k 15 (17); repeat from * across, ending with k 7 (8).

✳ Row 3: k 6 (7), *k2tog, k 14 (15), slip 1, k 1, pass slipped st over the knit st, k 14 (15); repeat from * across, ending with k 8 (9).

✳ Continue decreasing in this manner, maintaining stockinette stitch, until 12 sts remain. Bind off all sts, end yarn, leaving a long tail.

To finish:

✳ Sew up back seam. With long tail, thread tail through last 12 sts and pull tight. Weave in ends.

✳ To add a racing stripe of color in the ribbing, add the color 2 inches (5 cm) into the ribbing and work for 3 rows in the contrasting color. To add a colored stripe in the body of the hat, work 3 rows in st st after the rib and then work 3 rows in the contrasting color.

* Pattern by Candi Jensen

Wrap Creatively

Repurposed wraps are guilt-free and keep on giving.

A gorgeous wrap gives almost as much enjoyment as the gift itself. Store-bought wrap is far from eco-friendly, unless you find recycled wrap, and not at all personal. There are lots of greener, more creative wrapping options to try.

PAPER

Paper remains a top-notch wrapping material, but the planet will thank you for avoiding store-bought Christmas papers and paraphernalia. Here are some greener alternatives.

Past Christmases wrap: Keep all the lovely shiny, textured, multicolored, high-design, Christmas-themed paper that people have used to wrap their gifts to you. You can smooth it out and store on or in empty cardboard tubes. Don't forget to keep the tissue paper from gift boxes, too. Reuse as wrapping paper with a twist—layer it, recombine pieces into a new wrap, or make a collage.

Brown paper bags: They are sturdy, and when cut open, can be quite large. Customize with paint, stamps, decoupage, or crayon. Prettify with ribbon.

Glossy magazine paper: A golden resource for wrapping, beautiful, colorful pages make unique wraps. Tape or glue pages together or cut out just the images and words you like and glue them onto a brown paper bag.

Newspaper: A versatile gift wrap, the pages are large and can cover big packages easily. Try placing the crossword puzzle at the top for the wordsmith, or use the cartoon pages for kids. Look for newspapers in different languages, too. Use as is, or decorate as desired.

Old maps: Though no longer used for good directions, they make ideal gift wrap, being both visually interesting and large enough to cover a big gift.

Rolls of unused wallpaper: They get a second life by wrapping your packages.

Kids' art: Works that aren't framed or hanging on your fridge makes great wrapping paper; it also gives the young artist recognition and green points.

FABRIC

Versatile and reusable, fabric makes a splendid holiday wrap.

Remnants: If you do any sewing, you've got plenty of remnants lying around. Wrap up your package with this colorful alternative and tie it up with ribbon.

Leftover felt from other projects (see Felt Card, page 17): It's a fun and textured material for wrapping kids' presents that can be used to create other projects.

Repurposed sleeves or legs from shirts or pants: If too tattered to donate to charity, clothing is perfect for wrapping small gifts; tie the ends off with a "ribbon" strip cut from the body of the garment.

Extra dish towels or napkins lying around the house: Ones that haven't seen too much wear and tear can be given new life as gift wrap.

Furoshiki: This traditional Japanese technique of folding fabric is not only beautiful but also quite practical. Try this easy wrap—you can use any square of fabric, from a vintage scarf to a sewing remnant.

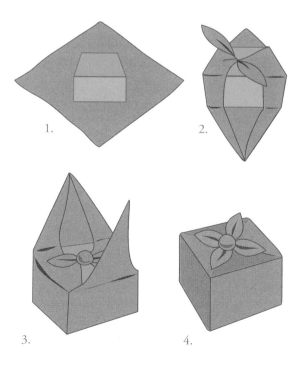

1.

2.

3.

4.

chapter

FIVE

CELEBRATING

Gatherings are at the very heart of celebrating Christmas, which finds its true meaning in bringing people together.

Sharing time with people you care about is what makes Christmas meaningful. The holidays afford plenty of opportunities for getting together to make merry, be thankful, and celebrate the warmth and camaraderie of the season. Like Christmas gifts, celebrations come wrapped in different packages, from small and intimate to large and boisterous, and everything in between. Adding a homemade touch to any celebration will make it more meaningful for you and your guests. In this chapter, you'll find a wealth of ideas for different ways to celebrate, and suggestions for party themes that will lend any event extra flair.

✳

You can host a traditional holiday party at home, whether it's an all-day open house for everyone you know or an intimate gathering of your closest friends for a night of nostalgic holiday viewing. Or gather your friends and neighbors together for a craft bazaar where everyone can sell their homemade wares, as well as accomplish some holiday shopping. Why not host a giving party, where everyone brings and leaves with a gift, a variation of White Elephant and Secret Santa games?

✳

If your home is too small for many guests, consider organizing an outing—attend the local Christmas spectacular, look at stores' holiday window displays or your neighbors' fabulous lighting extravaganzas, go to a show or recital, or set up a caroling party complete with lyric cheat-sheet cards for all.

✻

Homemade favors, decorations, and goodies will make your festivity extra memorable. Projects in this chapter include handcrafted place cards, Christmas crackers, and an easy, nature-inspired homemade centerpiece.

✻

Another way to give of yourself is to volunteer in your community, sharing goodwill with those less fortunate.

✻

Make the effort to carry out your family traditions or start new ones that you think are fun—read a Christmas story aloud, bring a freshly baked loaf to a neighbor, or take a Christmas day stroll through a nearby park. Whatever activity you choose, the very act of repeating it each year guarantees warm holiday memories.

Give a Giving Party

Get everyone together for a fun gift exchange.

Family members near and far, friends, colleagues. . . when you count up all the people you have to find gifts for, the length of the list can be intimidating. To simplify the process, cut costs, and find a fun way to connect with one another, consider playing some of these giving games.

WHITE ELEPHANT PARTY

The classic white elephant party works both for big groups and intimate gatherings. Each person goes home with a present, so long as they bring a present. A typical white elephant party is lively and can even get raucous. The rules are simple.

1. Ask each of your guests to bring a wrapped, unlabeled gift. Make the theme "homemade," and give invites.

2. Place all the gifts on a central table. Each person draws a number to establish the order for choosing a gift.

3. The first person selects a gift from the pile and opens it in front of everyone. (Everyone should feel free to exclaim and comment.)

4. The next person has the option to choose another gift from the pile or steal the first person's gift. If number two opts to steal the gift, the first person gets to choose and open another gift from the pile.

5. The third person has the option of opening a wrapped gift or stealing from either of the first two people, and so on, until everyone has an opened gift. You may wish to set a "theft limit," i.e., no gift may change hands more than three times.

6. At least one gift is sure to be wanted by multiple people; competition for the coveted item promises to be the most entertaining part of the game!

> If you want to make the game more challenging, try choosing a more complicated theme. For example, all gifts must be a certain color or include a specific ingredient.

SECRET SANTA PARTY

Great for large families, groups of friends, and work associates. The object of a secret Santa party is to keep your secret while trying to figure out the identity of your own secret Santa. Here are the rules.

1. Write the names of everyone who will be participating on separate pieces of paper.

2. Place the names in a bag or a hat, and have each person draw a name. The name you draw is the person you have to buy a gift for.

3. Specify homemade or, if store-bought is okay, set cost limits for the gifts (e.g., under $10, between $20 and $30, and so on). You can also set a theme, such as "gifts for the kitchen" or "musical presents."

4. Make a date for the near future when you'll meet to exchange gifts.

5. Guests should wrap their gifts and label them with the recipient's name—decide in advance whether secret Santas will remain incognito or reveal themselves.

6. Get everyone together for the gift exchange, where surprises are sure to be plentiful!

For those who have family members and friends spread out around the country (and sometimes far-flung parts of the world), the game can still be played, but one person has to assume the role of the organizer.

1. Prepare a set of envelopes with the names and addresses of all the participating members.

2. Write the names on separate pieces of paper.

3. Ask a friend to pick names and place them in an envelope (make sure people don't get their own names).

4. Pick your recipient last. Seal and send out the envelopes.

5. Consider a conference call, video chat, or group message to connect.

Throw a Theme Party

Make your holiday party unique by giving it a theme.

Hosting a holiday party is a great way to connect with those you care about. Whether you decide to hold a small, elegant cocktail party or a lively all-ages bash, consider giving your party a theme. A theme has the added benefit of giving shy guests something to talk about with other guests and everyone something to focus their energy on.

Christmas sweater party: A costume party of sorts, for which the host requests that all guests wear the craziest Christmas sweater they can get their hands on. Hand out a prize at the end of the night for the "Best Christmas Sweater." You know the one—covered with appliqués of Santa and his elves, a snowman made of sequins, or dancing hot-pink gingerbread people. Your guests will have instant fodder for conversation as they recount where and when they acquired the garment.

Craft bazaar: If you or your friends are especially crafty, this is a great party that combines socializing, shopping, and maybe even earning a few extra holiday cents. Set up tables in your home where your friends can display their wares and let the browsing begin. Make sure to invite lots of friends for maximum sell-out!

Make-it-and-take-it party: Making stuff—gifts, ornaments, cookies, jewelry, wreaths, or whatever else you can think of—is much more fun when done in groups. And, of course, everyone goes home with something new. Add food and drinks, and you've got a party! Set aside an afternoon or evening and ask everyone to bring material for the project. If you end up finishing early, you can even tackle some wrapping.

Tree-trimming party: Your ornaments are out of storage and the strings of lights are untangled and in working order. All that's left to do is decorate—the perfect excuse to gather your friends and family together to eat, drink, and be merry. Make sure everyone has a chance to hang an ornament on the tree, and give the honor of placing the tree topper to the youngest person in the room.

Good cause party: In lieu of your guests bringing a bottle of wine or a food item for the party at hand, ask them to contribute canned food, dry goods, gently used coats, new toys, or cash donations that you can deliver to the organization of your choice.

Fondue party: The communal dish from Switzerland is a proven party pleaser. If you don't already have a fondue set handed down from your parents' 1970s heyday, you should be able to find one at the local thrift store—though it may be avocado green. Offer a savory option—the traditional melted cheese—using bread as your dipper. Then move on to everyone's favorite: the sweet fondue. Make sure to have plenty of fruit on hand (cut up into bite-size pieces) to dip into melted chocolate, honey, caramel, or marshmallow.

Christmas special party: Before VCRs and DVRs, watching your favorite Christmas cartoon or show was a highly anticipated event. The special was aired only one night a year, and if you missed it, you had to wait an entire year until it aired again. Re-create that feeling of anticipation and invite your friends over to watch a classic holiday cartoon or movie that was a favorite in your youth.

Dress-up party: Break out your best party finery and invite your friends to get decked out to the nines. Serve up retro cocktails and hors d'oeuvres, turn up the music, and let the dancing commence.

Christmas luau: With Bing Crosby and the Andrews Sisters' version of "Mele Kalikimaka" playing in the background, hand out colorful leis, mix up tropical cocktails, and transport your guests to a warmer climate for the night.

Kids-are-welcome party: If the wee ones are invited, keep them busy with cookie decorating (see page 60) or an easy craft, like making an ornament (see page 44). Or try playing traditional party games with a holiday twist: "Pin the Red Nose on the Rudolph" or "Musical Sleds," anyone?

Cookie exchange party: Each guest brings a plate of their favorite homemade cookies, all to be displayed on a table. Each guest also brings an empty container, in which they get to collect several samples of each cookie. Ask guests to share any stories about their cookies—and recipes, too!

Create Handmade Place Settings

A handmade favor, even of the simplest sort, adds a festive touch to the table.

A Christmas celebration calls for setting a special table. Try one of these simple projects to add a homemade touch to your holiday tabletop.

CHRISTMAS CRACKERS*

A tradition in the United Kingdom since the mid-nineteenth century, a Christmas cracker adds a pop to Christmas dinner. The cracker itself is a cardboard tube wrapped in tissue paper to resemble the wrapping of a bon-bon with its twisted ends. Pull on each end, and the cracker splits open with the sound of a pop or a crack. The contents of a traditional cracker include a tissue paper crown, a trinket, and a joke or trivia. Here's how to make your own crackers.

1. Collect empty cardboard toilet paper and paper towel tubes.

2. Each cracker will need one 4-inch (10 cm) tube for the center of the wrapping and two 2-inch (5 cm) tubes to simulate the twisted ends.

3. Cut your tissue paper or thin wrapping paper to a length of 10 inches (25 cm). The width should be enough to cover your tubes at least twice.

4. (Optional step) If you want the pop, lay a cracker snap (it looks like a thin piece of cardboard and can be ordered online) horizontally in the middle of the paper.

5. Lay the tubes horizontally at the bottom edge of your paper, spaced 2 inches (5 cm) apart. Slowly turn the tubes and the paper upward until completely rolled.

6. Pinch the 2-inch (5 cm) space between the center tube and one of the end tubes and tie it off with curling ribbon.

7. Leaving the other end open, insert your trinkets, tchotchkes, and notes into the center tube.

8. Tie off the other end with curling ribbon, and you now have a sweet place-setting decoration.

PLACE-SETTING SPRIGS

These sweet and tiny bouquets can be made from boughs trimmed from the tree or gathered while on a winter walk. Encourage your guests to take them home and reuse them as part of their own Christmas décor. You'll need some lengths of colored fabric ribbon, mini rubber bands, card stock, and small evergreen boughs.

1. Handwrite or print out each guest's name on a strip of card stock, and poke a tiny hole in the end.

2. Trim your boughs so they are roughly the same size, then gather into a small bouquet. Secure with the rubber band. Repeat for each guest.

3. Wrap the ribbon around the sprig to hide the rubber band. Leave tails long enough to slip through the hole in the name tag, and tie off.

PINECONE CENTERPIECE

This is a perfect example of a homemade touch that requires only moments of effort yet yields an outsize reward. All you need is that old silver bowl sitting in the back of your cupboard and a mound of pinecones. If nature doesn't supply these, you can find them at craft stores.

1. Line your bowl with a festive napkin or cloth. An alternative is pine boughs or other greenery.

2. Place the pinecones inside. Form a nice shape, and be sure the cones are securely situated so they don't roll away if a guest jostles the table during dinner.

*Project by Chica and Jo

Enjoy Local Christmas Pageantry

Revel in your community's Christmas spirit by attending local events.

In most communities, the holiday season yields a full schedule of public activities, from concerts to tree-lighting ceremonies, including plenty of free events. Make a point of choosing one or more to attend (make sure to get any necessary tickets in advance) as a special outing that can become an annual tradition. Choose something that will be meaningful, be it dinner and a show or a visit to the local department store to gaze at the lovely window displays and sit on Santa's lap. It will give everyone something to remember and to look forward to next year.

Ballet and theater: Classics of the season include *The Nutcracker*; Dickens' masterpiece, *A Christmas Carol*; and Handel's *Messiah*. Consider smaller theater or dance troupes' performances, as well as those put on by big companies.

School and church recitals: Enjoy and support the arts in your local community by attending a performance of holiday music, drama, or dance by local schoolchildren. Music and drama teachers look forward to this time of year and are certain to put on an enjoyable show.

Chorales, church choirs, and symphonies: Relish the angelic voices and graceful playing of local musicians, whether it's a set of your favorite holiday classics or a seventeenth-century Christmas concerto you're experiencing for the first time.

Cinema: Even though a lot of classic Christmas movies are shown on television throughout the season, seeing a movie on the big screen is always enjoyable. Find out if your local cinema will be hosting special holiday screenings.

Museums: Museums often have special holiday exhibitions and events. Keep an eye out for designated days when the admission fee is waived for everyone or kids.

Tree-lighting ceremony: Most towns and cities host a tree-lighting ceremony in early December, when locals can gather to watch a larger-than-life tree brighten the night sky and unofficially mark the start of the holiday season.

Christmas market: The business districts in many communities often organize an all-day event when local businesses offer store discounts, free drinks and eats, special events for children, and musical entertainment.

Arts-and-crafts fairs: Buy one-of-a-kind gifts and support local artisans at a craft fair.

Historic open house tour: Have you always wanted to see the inside of those lovely historic homes in your town? Be on the lookout for an organized tour of the historic district, when the owners open their homes to the public to showcase their holiday décor.

Jingle bells fun run: Support a cause you believe in and work off the party food by tying on your running shoes and participating in a local 5k run. At most events, walkers are also welcome to participate. Not only will you be helping a good cause and getting some exercise, but you will also receive a T-shirt to commemorate your participation in the event.

Festival of lights: Pile the kids into the car or jump on the bus and visit the neighborhood in your community known for having the most extravagant outdoor displays of Christmas decoration and lights. An evening of viewing will even get the biggest Scrooge into the holiday spirit.

Botanical gardens and public parks: Many local green spaces offer special holiday-themed exhibits and workshops or wildlife walks. Get the family together for some local nature appreciation or outdoor time.

> If you cannot go out to see a holiday performance, you can organize one of your own at home by putting on a Christmas play with the kids. Re-enact your favorite holiday play, movie, or musical or come up with your own script, get out the dress-up clothes, and put on the stage makeup. Send out invitations to the family, then it's time for lights, camera, action! Don't forget to record it for posterity.

Watch a Christmas Classic

Even if you've seen a movie, cartoon, or television show multiple times, it's still satisfying to watch your favorite characters tackle their individual conflicts and discover the true meaning of Christmas.

We'll never forget the moment when George Bailey returns home, after seeing what life would be like without him, delirious with happiness and gratitude in *It's a Wonderful Life*. Or when Ralphie's wish comes true in *A Christmas Story*—a Red Ryder BB gun!—and, just as his mother predicts, he almost shoots his eye out. Gather the family and make watching one of these funny, sentimental, and heartwarming moments together an essential part of your Christmas ritual.

THE CLASSICS

∗ *A Christmas Carol:* Charles Dickens's story of old Ebenezer Scrooge, who learns about the spirit of generosity by being led through his past, present, and future by three ghosts. A multitude of film versions have been made; here is a quick guide to some of the more popular ones.

   ∗ *A Christmas Carol* (1938): An early Hollywood adaptation

   ∗ *Scrooge* (1970): A musical

   ∗ *Scrooged* (1988): A modern take on the story

   ∗ *A Christmas Carol* (1999): A made-for-television version

∗ *Holiday Inn* (1942): The musical film that introduced Irving Berlin's "White Christmas" to the world.

∗ *Meet Me in St. Louis* (1944): Though not entirely about the holidays, this film does feature Judy Garland's very touching rendition of "Have Yourself a Merry Little Christmas."

∗ *It's a Wonderful Life* (1946): One of the most beloved films of all time is Frank Capra's story of George Bailey, a beleaguered businessman on the brink of suicide who's given a preview of what life would be if he'd never been born.

∗ *Miracle on 34th Street* (1947): Starring a young Natalie Wood, this movie lets you believe there really is a Santa Claus.

✳ *White Christmas* (1954): This follow-up to *Holiday Inn* stars the dynamic duo of Bing Crosby and Danny Kaye.

MODERN CLASSICS

✳ *A Christmas Story* (1983): The sweet, sentimental story—set in the 1940s—of Ralphie Parker, his family and friends, and his wild fantasies of a BB gun.

✳ *National Lampoon's Christmas Vacation* (1989): Chevy Chase stars in this holiday romp.

✳ *The Nightmare Before Christmas* (1993): Tim Burton's animated, unusual, and fantastical take on the holiday.

✳ *Elf* (2003): In this sweet comedy, a human raised as a North Pole elf sets out to find his biological father in New York City.

✳ *Fred Claus* (2007): Santa's older, begrudging brother, who's forced to move to the North Pole to take over the operations, finally sees the magic of the season.

CHILDREN'S FAVORITES

✳ *Rudolph, the Red-Nosed Reindeer* (1964): The animated story of a misfit reindeer who is discovered by Santa Claus in the North Pole and needs Rudolph's shining beacon to guide his way.

✳ *A Charlie Brown Christmas* (1965): The story of hapless Charlie Brown, the lovable cartoon character created by Charles Schulz, who is in search of the true meaning of Christmas.

✳ *How the Grinch Stole Christmas!* (1966): The classic book's cartoon adaptation of the cold and bitter creature—with a heart that's "two sizes two small"—who tries to ruin Christmas for the Whos of Whoville.

✳ *Emmet Otter's Jug-Band Christmas* (1977): Jim Henson's musical take on O. Henry's "The Gift of the Magi" about a poor otter family and the risks they take to win a Christmas Eve talent contest.

✳ *Home Alone* (1990): Starring Macaulay Culkin, a young boy who is accidentally left behind has to protect his home from a pair of conniving thieves.

Go Caroling

Singing together fosters a sense of harmony.

Christmas songs have a way of edging into all aspects of our lives during the holidays. You'll hear them in stores, on the radio in the car, in elevators, in the doctor's office, and on the street. Before you know it, you're singing right along! This year, enjoy those songs by bringing together your family, friends, and neighbors to form a chorus of carolers.

* Gather a small group, then go house to house in your neighborhood and belt out tunes for the neighbors.

* If you have a piano at home and know someone who can tickle those ivories, plan an evening to gather 'round and sing together.

* Bring the music to your local senior center, hospital, or other community center. Offer to escort your child's school class on a community caroling expedition.

* For those who prefer the limelight, set up a karaoke machine and serenade the revelers. Just be sure to share the microphone.

* Carols aren't just for singing! Amateur musicians can polish up their brass instruments or fire up their electric guitars and entertain crowds with their holiday renditions.

* If you've always enjoyed singing, it might just be the perfect time of the year to commit to joining a church choir or a community chorale group.

O TANNENBAUM

Make copies of the lyrics for your singers to share; a handmade Christmas songbook bound with red yarn makes a useful keepsake.

Volunteer

Create some homemade goodwill when you give back to the community.

Most of us are blessed with the basic necessities of living—and much more—but there are individuals and families who can benefit from your time and effort, especially during the holidays. Volunteer your time and help get supplies, shelter, food, and whatever else to those in need faster. Here are a few simple ways you can help out in your community.

Find a local soup kitchen or shelter: Help out in whatever way the organization needs most. You might be boxing up packages, serving food, cleaning up after the meal, delivering meals, or helping in the office.

Offer your professional services gratis: Whether you're a physician, architect, accountant, public relations expert, lawyer, or teacher, find an organization that can benefit from your expertise.

Fundraise: Most non-profit organizations and charities need fundraising help. Offer to make phone calls and send emails soliciting donations.

Read aloud: Your local library, school, hospital, or seniors' home will eagerly accept your offer to read aloud.

Improve your neighborhood: Many public parks, beaches, and community gardens hold clean-up days—get out and improve your neighborhood.

Organize a swap: Toys, clothing, books, CDs, Halloween costumes, and sports equipment are just a few things that folks can happily exchange at a swap meet. Do a specific theme or a jumble.

> Organizations such as idealist.org and volunteer.gov will match your skills and time to a local or international volunteer opportunity.

kid friendly # Read a Christmas Tale

Start a new tradition of holiday story nights, and let each member of the family choose a story to read aloud.

Reading together is a wonderful way to connect and to rediscover the spirit of the holiday. And it's not just for families with young children—the pleasure of hearing a story read aloud transcends all ages.

✷ Designate one evening per week in December to be family story night. The reader for that evening chooses the book or story to read from, and everyone gathers to hear the tale. Have fun with it, making up voices for the characters or even acting out scenes in dramatic fashion.

✷ Invite the younger neighborhood kids over one morning or afternoon in December for a read-aloud event or offer to organize a similar event at your local library. Their parents will be grateful to have a few free hours to do some shopping or wrapping.

✷ Listening to audiobooks, podcasts, and even radio is another great way for your family to participate in the oral storytelling tradition. Whether it's the author or a professional actor reading the words, it will surely be enjoyable and unforgettable.

✷ Even if you don't have the time to participate in a book club throughout the year, make a holiday and social event of it by choosing a great Christmas book to read and discuss with your friends over festive food and drink.

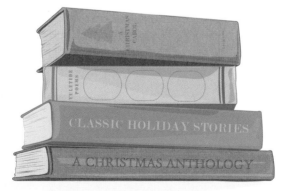

PICTURE BOOKS

* *How the Grinch Stole Christmas!* by Dr. Seuss
* *The Polar Express* by Chris Van Allsburg
* *Olive, the Other Reindeer* by Vivian Walsh & J. Otto Seibold
* *Mr. Willowby's Christmas Tree* by Robert Barry
* *The Christmas Miracle* of *Jonathan Toomey* by Susan Wojciechowski & P. J. Lynch
* *The Sweet Smell of Christmas* by Patricia M. Scarry & J. P. Miller (scratch and sniff)
* *The 12 Days of Christmas* by Robert Sabuda (pop-up)

If the number of holiday titles to choose from seems overwhelming, stick to the classics, or look for a Christmas-themed book that is part of a series or has a character your child enjoys.

SHORT STORIES, NOVELS, & POEMS

* "The Night Before Christmas" by Clement C. Moore
* "The Gift of the Magi" by O. Henry
* *A Christmas Carol* by Charles Dickens
* "A Child's Christmas in Wales" by Dylan Thomas
* "A Christmas Memory" by Truman Capote
* *Letters from Father Christmas* by J. R. R. Tolkien
* *Christmas Day in the Morning* by Pearl S. Buck
* *The Best Christmas Pageant Ever* by Barbara Robinson

MISCELLANEOUS FOR ADULTS

* *Holidays on Ice* by David Sedaris (humor)
* *Hercules Poirot's Christmas* by Agatha Christie (mystery)
* *A Redbird Christmas* by Fannie Flagg (fiction)
* *The Battle for Christmas* by Stephen Nissenbaum (history)
* *The Haunted Tea-Cosy* by Edward Gorey (graphic novel)
* *When Christmas Comes* by Debbie Macomber (romance)

Organize a Christmas Day Activity

Make Christmas Day about more than just gifts and food by organizing a special afternoon event that can become a family tradition.

On Christmas Day, once the dust has settled from all the presents being opened, the wrapping paper has been sorted, and everyone is satiated from a great brunch (see page 73)—in the lull before dinner—try engaging in some fun activities. Don't forget to take pictures!

If the weather outside is not frightful, inspire the family to get out and enjoy the brisk winter air (or warm breezes, if you live in a southerly climate) with these vigorous activities.

Winter sports: It's the perfect time of year for ice skating, downhill or cross-country skiing, sledding, snowshoeing, and playing in the snow.

Bike riding: If the wind isn't too brisk, pull out the bikes for a languorous excursion, a destination ride, or just a jaunt around the neighborhood.

Touch football: Instead of watching football on television, split up your family and friends into two teams for a gentler version of the game.

Hiking or walking: You don't need to be in the mountains to go on a pleasant walk. Consider the beach, a park, a forest reserve, or a few city blocks.

If the weather refuses to cooperate with your plans, here are a few ideas to pass the time indoors.

Play games: Board games, charades, bingo, jigsaw puzzles, and cards are only the tip of the iceberg. Give the family a new game each Christmas for the purpose of playing on this day.

Watch old home movies or look at family photos: Whether they're memories from the past or present, Christmas day is a great time for reminiscing about those who are near and far.

Have a dance party: Designate a different DJ each year to make a playlist, spin the tunes, and get the party started.

Karaoke: Getting tired of Christmas tunes? Let your inner diva shine while singing your favorite non-holiday songs.

kid friendly Wish Your Neighbors a Happy Holiday

Delicious baked goods make for excellent neighborly relations.

Start a new tradition in your neighborhood by baking batches of scones, cookies, or another goodie and dropping them off at your neighbors' homes. Whether it's your secret family recipe for amazing cranberry-lemon scones, brownies made from a box, or store-bought pastries, the point is to spread goodwill and cheer among your neighbors and wish them a happy holiday. Even a small treat can create a lot of warm feelings. Here are some ideas for easy-baked gifts.

* Cookies (recipes on pages 58 and 59)
* Lemon bars
* Banana, zucchini, or pumpkin bread (recipe on page 55)
* Fruit scones
* Brownies
* Cinnamon buns
* Croissants
* Cupcakes
* Coffee cake
* Truffles (recipe on page 62)

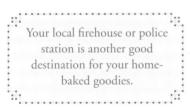

Your local firehouse or police station is another good destination for your home-baked goodies.

RESOURCES

INDEX

ABOUT THE AUTHOR

Tina Barseghian is a San Francisco Bay Area-based writer, editor, author, and blogger. After working at *ReadyMade* and *Craft* magazines, writing a DIY design blog, and authoring the book *Get a Hobby! 101 All-Consuming Diversions for Every Lifestyle*, she's learned a thing or two about making things by hand. By far the most important lesson: Have fun and enjoy the process.

ABOUT THE ILLUSTRATOR

Alison Kendall is a freelance artist, graphic designer, and marine biologist, currently living and working in San Francisco. In addition to working on various design and illustration projects, she has been a regular designer for *MAKE* and *Craft* magazines since 2007.

ACKNOWLEDGMENTS

Thanks to all who collaborated with me on this book, including artist extraordinaire Alison Kendall, Candi Jensen, Maggie Pace, Daelyn Short, Diane Gilleland, Tom Cavers, Heather Coppersmith, Christopher Coppersmith, David Noller, Diane Hiatt, Chica and Jo, Lynne Yeamans, Tanya Ross-Hughes, Tiffany Threadgould, Nanette Blum, and my patient editor, Erin Canning. Also thanks to Deb Brody and Alex Colon at Harlequin and Sharyn Rosart at Quirk. Finally, I'm grateful to my husband, Lloyd, and daughter, Lucy, who helped prototype many of the projects and recipes for this book.